You Will Win

You Will Win

Jekalyn Carr

Trilogy Christian Publishing

You were "CREATED TO WIN"

Your "WINNING SEASON" is not compared to the four seasons of the earth;
summer, fall, winter or spring, but it is a set time of being victorious.

"IT'S A SEASON THAT'S LASTS A LIFETIME".
"ENJOY YOUR LIFETIME OF WINNING"
"FAILURE IS NOT IN YOUR DNA"
"YOU HAVE WINNING WORDS OVER YOUR LIFE"
"YOU ARE A CHAMPION"
"GOD DON'T BIRTH NO FAILURES"
"SPEAK SUCCESS"
"GREATER IS COMING"
"SOMETHING BIG IS HAPPENING"
"LIVE BEYOND YOUR PAST"
"YOUR FUTURE IS A WINNING FUTURE"

THE MESSAGE BEHIND
YOU WILL WIN

While traveling, I began to listen to the testimonies of many. It seemed as if the individuals were functioning in a position of defeat. People situations – whether it was their finances, careers, relationships, health, or whatsoever they were presently up against, were winning over them when it should be the reverse. So, I began to earnestly pray to God, and seek Him on what He would have me declare to His people. That is to say, the Lord gave me the message, "You Will Win," to remind His people across the world that He doesn't create failures, He creates champions. God has assured us victory over all circumstances. Throughout this message, I want to assist people to unleash the champion that's within them.

It's not God's intention to see His people defeated. In life, you sometimes realize as God begins to shift us towards greater levels and dimensions, the greater the level, the greater the giant. However, one thing we must remember that it doesn't matter how enormous the giant may appear to be; we must be aware of who we are and recognize the power

God has given us over the enemy, we are then equipped to FIGHT TO WIN instead of FEARING TO LOSE! God began to reveal how it doesn't necessitate a giant to defeat a giant. Whatever character your "giant" has taken in your life, whether it be a disappointment, misfortune, illness, etc., "You Will Win" allows us to know there is something within us that's going to promote us to win this season!

We must understand that anytime we are living and functioning as the opposite of who God has created us to be, we are living under a false identity. When we assume the names or the characteristics of anything other than the victorious children of God, we are not operating in the fullness of God's grace, deliverance, and power. If you are living in defeat, you are living under a false identity.

One thing that is pivotal to know on our journey to win is when defeat calls, we don't have to answer. When failure is calling, we don't have to respond. Why? Because that's not who we are! That's not who or what God calls us; He calls us a CHAMPION. It must dwell in our spirit that we are the children of the most grandest champion, Jesus! So as His children, if He has created us in His image and likeness, somewhere within us lies a champion. Losing is not even in our DNA!

"You Will Win" is a message to encourage you to cease from answering the wrong voice. Therefore, we must stop allowing the enemy to steal our victory. A real champion never enjoy the continuation of feeling overwhelmed. "You Will Win" challenges us to lay our hands on everything in our lives that appears overwhelming and COMMAND it to WIN!

You have the power and the authority to speak to your SEASON and declare that you will NEVER have a season of defeat again because you are a WINNER! Throughout the day, you must frequently declare "*I WILL WIN*," for the message to enter into your heart. Before you know it, by repeatedly speaking this declaration to yourself and your life, you will start performing and living like the winner, you were destined to be! I encourage you not only keep this declaration to yourself, but instead, release it to everyone you know who's living in positions of defeat.

YOU WILL WIN! YOU WILL WIN! YOU WILL WIN!

DEDICATION

I dedicate this book to YOU!
You, who have ever felt defeated…
You, who have ever felt like giving up…
You, who have ever felt like the load was too heavy,
and the obstacle was too great…
You, who have considered throwing in the towel…
To every dreamer…
To every fighter…
To every person on the frontlines of their battles…
God gave me these words to push you to "win." It is my desire, that
you grasp the messages herein, and they inspire you to take your rightful
place as a CHAMPION.
This win is for you!

ACKNOWLEDGEMENTS

I would like to acknowledge the following individuals, groups, and organizations for their unwavering prayers, support, and encouragement that has made this – my first book – a reality:

To God, thank You for entrusting this profound message to me. Thank You for a reminder of the victory that is inevitable in YOU! Thank You for the grace and mercy you continuously extend to us, Your children. Thank You for depositing, within us, all that we need to live victoriously. Thank you for every person who reads these pages. May your love, comfort, and peace, be with them now and always.

To my parents, I am eternally indebted to you for the love, guidance, sacrifices, and the inspiration you continually provide. I could not do any of this without you and I truly thank God for you both. To my family, thank you for your support, which has allowed me to journey all over the world carrying the messages God gives me. Many times, your lives have been impacted and affected by my calling and I am grateful for the grace and the love that you consistently show. I love you all.

To the Music industry, that has helped me to minister to another faction of God's people, via written inspiration. For all the years of support, encouragement, and prayers, I thank you from the bottom of my heart.

To TBN Publishing, thank you for believing in my gifts, and in what God has deposited inside of me for His people. Thank you for allowing me the opportunity to align with your sacred mission to spread the love and word of Jesus Christ with the world! The work you do, and the lives you touch are immeasurable. I thank God for you, and for allowing our ministries to intersect in such a profound and poignant way.

To the readers of this book, thank you for your continued support of my vision, and trusting me to carry and convey everything God has positioned inside me, for you.

Thank you for joining me on this journey from singer to author. I am a living testament that with Christ, all things are possible. It is my sincere and humble prayer that everything you read on these pages irrevocably impact your life, and ignite a fire within you that cannot be extinguished, and that your hearts and lives will forever be changed by the message of victory!

CONTENTS

INTRODUCTION

I can attest to the "winning attitude" that my family and I had to have. I've gone from singing with the back porch as my stage and the grass as my audience, to becoming a major independent recording artist, receiving a Grammy nomination, two Billboard Music Award nominations, a Stellar Award, and being honored by Ebony Magazine as a member of the Power 100, among countless other achievements and accolades. I was able to have these experiences before I finished my teens. I received many invitations, but I couldn't accept them all. The demand was great and overwhelming, but it was a good overwhelming. The "winning attitude" that we had to carry when others didn't believe in what we were doing had a major impact on our success. My family knew my passion was and is to inspire and bless others. Therefore, it took a "winning attitude" for my dad to leave the corporate world to enter a world that was distinct. My family encouraged me to win and informed me that I could be anything that I wanted to be in life. Those words intensified my winning spirit at an early age up to now. It took the right attitude for me to put in writing my observations and challenges which rendered my first book.

In this book, I want to contribute to you my thoughts, understanding, and testimony on what it takes to be a winner.

It's Your Winning Season! Not only is it your winning season, but Everything Attached To You Wins!

My new single, "You Will Win" was released on September 15, 2017. It is the lead song for my new album titled *One Nation Under God*.

One Nation Under God is a call for all of God's people to unite, removing the limitations of race, religion, denomination, organization, location, gender, and class.

With this new release, I address how God desires to see His people, and how we should view ourselves - as one united body of believers. God's love for us all is consistent. The same love, grace, and mercy that

He extends to one; He continues to all. My compassion has always been seeing the people of God blessed, walking in every promise that God has spoken over their lives. There is a powerful theme throughout *One Nation Under God*, as I focus on corporate worship and spiritual community. I pray this project helps to foster a global impact and remind believers that we are all connected. I feel compelled to reiterate that we, the people of God, are ONE body. No matter where we are, America, Africa, Russia, Canada, China, Australia, or any other place in this world we are all connected by the God we serve, and the grace that He has over our lives."

You can order any projects of mine on digital outlets such as: ITunes, Google Play, Amazon and many others. The hard copy can be bought at retail stores and online.

Albums	Released
One Nation Under God	2018
The Life Project	2016
It's Gonna Happen	2014
Greater Is Coming	2013
Promise	2010

THE CHALLENGE

Jekalyn's #YOUWILLWIN Social Media Challenge
I challenge you to enter with me into a new season that commands winning behavior and results for our lives. Take the #YOUWILLWIN Challenge:

Step 1: Join the Challenge
Repost the #YOUWILLWIN Challenge graphic on your
social media page with the caption below:
I am entering into a season of intentional winning in my life.
#YOUWILLWIN Challenge!
For the next 21 days
You can visit youwillwin.org to get the #youwillwin Challenge graphic.

Step 2: Wake up and Win
Read the selected scripture for the day. Engage in immediate prayer.

Step 3: Win
#YOUWILLWIN Challenge

iamjekalyncarr.com
youwillwin.org

"But thanks be to God, which giveth us the victory through our Lord Jesus Christ."
1 Corinthians 15:57

PRINCIPLE I:
INTENTIONAL VICTORY

There is no victory without intent to win.

"Winning" is an act of high intention. We must set our plan to win in motion from the start. My journey toward "winning" has been quite an experience, but every moment has been worth it. We are all winners. We were created to live a life of greatness. We must know the choices and strategies that we employ will bring us closer to winning ultimately and fulfilling our destiny.

To go through life without tapping into a plan or vision can leave a person not fulfilling their true destiny and reason of being here on earth. We are amazing genetically — molecules, cells, muscles, brain, etc. With all the different tissues and body parts that help to make men and women bodies, one of the most critical factors is the mind. It controls the function of how we perceive things, how we live, how we grow, and how we communicate. With the appropriate mindset, you can "win." In this book, I will be referring to our thoughts, mindset, words, and actions a great deal. These key components foster the course for your victory.

When I was younger, we believed God for many things to come to pass; I learned the first thing we had to do was see it before it happened. Once we thought it, we began to release the words through our mouths. By applying the expressions, by reflecting and then releasing them, we gained the faith to go after the things we believed God would provide. In this book, I will talk directly to you to persuade you toward your lifetime of winning.

Intentional Victory

When we aspire to win, we must be strategic. We must also recognize the patterns that God has set in motion for our lives and be clear that God created us uniquely. Thus, the path to righteousness and success is not a one size fits all. We must be clear in our ways and listen humbly to His directives for each of us.

I've also outlined several guiding principles that keep my heart, mind, and spirit set on winning, and I want to share them with you. To be a winner, you must think like a winner. In sports, you will find the one that wins the championship is the one who has winning thoughts. Your winning ideas motivate you in your drive to have success in your life. Yes, you must prepare yourself for the winning season, but most of all, your thoughts must be present. Your body can be well and fit by going through all the training, but if you don't have the will to succeed, you will not win.

Defining a Win

The way you define your success also determines your destiny.

Would you rather be a winner or a loser? I would imagine that most would answer they wish to be a winner. Becoming a winner leads me to the following questions: What does victory look like? How is a "win" defined? The dictionary defines a "win" as being "in a race or contest by who finishes first." It is imperative that we define success on our terms and most importantly by God's definition. Winning in the world and winning according to God's plan is, not the same. I define "wins" in my life through the completion of the orders given to me by God. I believe that victory constitutes God's will. The effort exerted in carrying out God's plan for our lives is a defining factor for a win. We must also consider that "win" is a verb. The act of winning consists of a constant state of motion that we engage in to meet the desired end.

The way that we decide to define "wins" and losses affects the overall outcome and what we believe we can attain in our lifetime.

When we first recognize ourselves as winners, creating a definition is much different. Wins can transpire at any point in our lives, and they calculate in a myriad of ways. When we consider God's constant motion in our lives, there is genuinely no loss. In sports, a contest, or awards event, people define a win by who gets the trophy or who won the title. I want you to understand me undoubtedly that's true in that world, but in our day-to-day lives winning is not exclusively about a trophy or plaque, but contentment in our lives, serenity in our homes, permanence, excellent health, serving one another, and I could continue the list of things.

Comparing your life to a game or event should not be your resolution. Your "win" centers around your daily victories. A person who's overcoming drugs and alcohol abuse is winning. Learning how to defeat your struggle is a win. When you have a person who operates very poorly on financial matters, and he or she begins to put aside $10 a week, that's a win. It's not the amount the person started with, but it's the starting practice, the effort to be better, makes it a "win."

Another example is when college students get delayed in their efforts because they haven't been applying themselves by hanging out to have fun. When they grasp that their grades are suffering, they understand something must change. The students then decide to decline their friends' requests to hang out for the weekend, settle in, and begin to prepare for improved grades. Responsibility is a win. They are applying themselves to what's important.

When a person says, "I'm going to lose weight because I am 45 pounds overweight or I want to change my life and be healthier," when a person makes up his or her mind, the individual is now beginning the winning process by losing weight week after week. Their husband or wife, family, and friends are encouraging and celebrating the progress and now seeing that individual have lost all the weight that you desired.

If that is your story, you have the right to celebrate this win because you have won. "Wins" come in all shapes and forms in our lives, and for many of us, it is a day-by-day win. You won't receive a trophy for every "win" in your life, but every "win" will bring you the happiness that you deserve in the short and long run. Do not compare your "wins" to your friends' or other people's victories. You may have several things in common, but you must never assess your wins by what others achieve. You may use them as a reference guide of some sort to create a win, but do not try to duplicate others' wins, because, in the long run, this type of action causes you to be unsuccessful.

Learn how to celebrate each win. Tell God, "Thank you!" and celebrate your accomplishments. You may not be able to have an out of this world party for every "win," but sometimes a victory shout or celebration dance for a few minutes is great. Just make sure you commemorate your "wins." I will explain more about celebrating your "wins" and what it does for you later in the book.

Celebrating a Win

After each win in your life whether it is big or small, take a moment and reflect on where you have come from and where you are now. By taking a moment to celebrate, you learn not to overlook accomplishments in your life. It also helps you value the "win" better. You must have a "winning attitude" even after you "win."

Learning to celebrate a "win" helps you say, "Now that I have accomplished this, what can I do next?" It motivates you to go after another "win" in your life. It's just like this: you work alongside your colleagues, and you excel in your work. That makes the whole team look good, but if no one acknowledges your great performance, over time, you will become stagnant and lose your drive. Celebrating your win is like that. If you don't acknowledge it, you will become complacent. You lose focus on how to have an appreciation for your accomplishments, and it will alter your view and vision of a "win." You will miss opportunities of laughter and enjoyment. You will miss opportunities to say, "Wow!"

My dad told me that in corporate America when something significant happened, they would take fifteen minutes to celebrate and get back to work. Everyday life should be the same, when you receive a promotion, pass a test, buy a new car, purchase a new home, learn how to ride a bike, learn how to balance your schedule or all the other great opportunities that you will have; you will need to celebrate.

I remember my family being thrilled to give more in tithes and offerings because God blessed us with more. That was a win for us. I also remember my family being able to sow into people's lives in times of need or in times when God placed it in our hearts to do so. We were pleased to help and plant because we were blessed. That was a win for my family. Many times we would reminisce about what good things happened, and we would laugh, shout, holler, run, and thank God for where we've come from and what we have accomplished. In those three to five minutes, or sometimes less or more depending on our time and place, we would celebrate and then get back to work. Celebrating a win sometimes mean breaking out cake and ice cream, but not always for smaller victories. I say, whether big or small, be sure to celebrate. Celebrating gives you the motivation for another win, and it also allows God to see you appreciate His blessings upon your life. Anytime you perform a kindness for someone, and they respond with a simple thank you, it makes you feel appreciated. With you appreciating your wins, it makes God feel good.

"Let the Lord be magnified, which hath pleasure in the prosperity of his servant." *Psalms 35:27 (KJV)*

Don't spend in excess of time celebrating yesterday's "win" or become complacent. You must look for other areas in your life where you can expand. Once you "win," remind yourself that if you accomplished a goal, then you can achieve your next goal. You are one more degree closer to your subsequent victory. Celebrating is effective when positioning yourself to accomplish your next "win." There is an old saying, "you can't win today's ballgame with yesterday's home run." You must be grateful for what you accomplished yesterday, but you must also step up to the base today and bat the ball until you hit and make a home run. Remember your "win" is what you define it as. Understanding your "winning" moments creates an atmosphere for a continuation of "wins." Celebrating is an essential key to keep moving forward.

Keep Winning

When you hear people talk about how successful they were in their past, often they have not completed anything notable since then. They may give the remarks of making it to the place of success and convinces themselves there's nothing more to be done but soon realizes they should have continued the journey to a more considerable success. Somewhere they achieved a momentous milestone and felt they had reached the ceiling of prosperity. When you give one victory in your life precedence over others, you accept that position without pursuing another win.

No, it is not the best decision to get settled on one win. It reduces your motivation, ambition, willpower, dedication, and tenacity to succeed. When you are running laps in a race, and you're the first one to finish the first lap, that is good, and yes, you can celebrate that moment, but if you discontinue running at the current lap because you were ahead; you will not finish the race. Life is like that after you finish the first lap, you must run the next and continue running the laps until you have completed the race.

Don't Overlook a Win

Here's a personal story I want to share to encourage you to understand the beauty of winning. Sometimes we will be derailed and miss the truth about winning. I remember saying I wanted to bless people with my gifts. The more people I touch, the more I help, and in return, our family and business are blessed. God allowed me to have such success at the age of 15 when my first prominent song "Greater Is Coming" was released. The song expanded across the world. The album debuted at Number three on Billboard's Top Gospel Albums chart. Right before my eyes, what I was pursuing was happening.

When my song, "You're Bigger" was released from "The Life Project" album, people expressed to me how it inspired and touched their lives. The song did very well across the world, as it climbed the music charts. At the age of 16, I received my first Stellar Award for the song "Greater Is Coming." My dreams continued at the age of 19, with life-changing award nominations. My award nominated song "You're Bigger" was nominated for a Grammy, two Billboard Awards, and several Stellar Awards. It remained in the top 10 on the Gospel Billboard chart for over 40 weeks, and it became the Number 1 song in gospel music on the charts. At the age of 19 within six months' time. I was asked to be a part of almost every major musical show that aired on television including the Triumph Awards Show, the Trumpet Award Show, Black Music Honors, BET Gospel Super Bowl, and Joyful Noise. I have experienced many beautiful desired blessed moments on this journey.

Testimonies were shared with me from across the world, declaring how this song rescued them. Choirs were singing it, and praise dancers were dancing to it.

The song, "You're Bigger" exceedingly blessed many people. I realized that, what I prayed for, God had given me at such a young age. By the time I reached 19, I had received a nomination for one of the biggest award in music. Even though I didn't win the awards, I learned not to overlook my accomplishment. My family and I created a legacy for me as an independent artist.

The awards would have felt great to win, but I received the true reward, and that was for years to come, knowing how blessed people are through the messages God has released through my family and me. I celebrate my accomplishments, and that is what "winning" is. It's all about how you define your happiness and your winning moment.

In this walk, you can't take on the attitude as a slacker when you feel the situations aren't going as planned. You must keep focused on what you are trying to attain even when it seems there aren't options that go your way. Sometimes what you were trying to accomplish, indeed was fulfilled, but it seems that it gets covered up with the distractions that came along with the accomplishments. I have seen many people disappointed because they felt things didn't entirely work out as they planned. At that moment, they assumed, they lost the battle, but circumstances redirected them.

Your setbacks may have forced you to embrace faith to launch your own business. They may have forced you to pull your family through unfavorable situations, return to school or write your first book.

Your setbacks may have also forced you not to quit or not to settle.

So, when you look at the bigger picture, some loses are not worth feeling bad over, but instead be thankful for what God has allowed you to accomplish in your life. Understand that "winning" is more prominent than one moment, one day, one event or one accomplishment. It's a word that we describe as a verb, which continues daily.

Having a "Winning Attitude"

I always knew that at some point God would do extraordinary things in my life, giving me huge opportunity after opportunity. Although I realized for me to have a successful and winning career, I had to think positively. I had to plant positive seeds in my mind first so that it could get embedded in my heart. I call it a "winning attitude." I made up my mind to refuse to lose in my career.

Why? Because losing is not even who I am, according to 2 Corinthians 2:14 KJV

"Now thanks be unto God, which always causeth us to triumph in Christ, and maketh manifest the savour of his knowledge by us in every place."

Being a loser is not who God created you to be. God has placed a great amount of potential in you, and when the enemy recognizes the fact that you now know it, he tries to send negative communication through your mind to make you devalue yourself. He will feed you messages like: "You will only go so far, you don't have what it takes to make it to the top, and you're not liked or noticed by anyone."

The enemy blindsides you with negative words to cause you to forget God doesn't make mistakes. When He created you, He made you *good*. I realized over time, what came with my "winning attitude" were phenomenal opportunities. God has given me opprotunities never in a million years did I think would happen.

I'll never forget the day I received the news that Ebony Magazine wanted to honor me in their Power 100, alongside people like Beyoncé, Lebron James, Pharrell Williams and so many other distinguished individuals. I find it interesting how God will always find a way to rebuild your confidence and belief in who He created you to be. That's not all! I remember when I was called to appear on several shows on television networks such as BET, TBN, IMPACT, OWN, and more! Because of my "winning attitude" not only did God give me tremendous opportunities but from those opportunities, He birthed out more significant conveniences, one after the other, including being featured in movies and television shows.

What if I allowed the negative words that was spoke contaminate the positive words I declared? You must understand that you cannot expect successful living with negative thinking. Your future, career, success, and your life, in general, deserve more. Even when you don't see anything happening that you forecasted would, such as doors opening in the timeframe you expected them to, you still must think and speak positively. You must have a "winning attitude." Sometimes we become worried, which eventually leads us to question ourselves, wondering are we good enough. We also question God, wondering if this is where He wants us positioned and is this what He called us to do.

I want you to understand that just because you don't notice anything happening in the natural, that does not mean God is not working in the spirit for you. If God has called you to it, He's going to carry you through it! Our Father, God, is waiting for that right moment to release you into "greater" and bigger success. Never give God the impression that He didn't know what He was doing when He created, called, and chose you. Don't put your career in the hands of the negativity and false information the enemy places in your mind to imprison you and your visions. Keep your "winning attitude" because it blocks the enemy.

Most successful people became that way because of the "winning attitudes" they carry. Their "winning attitude" is referred to as their push, drive, passion, and eagerness to learn and succeed. Most winning people did not grow up with a silver spoon in their mouths. Their success doesn't come from the fact that they had a great idea, it was what they did with the idea. Their attitude and passion for their vision made them successful.

One familiar example of someone with a "winning attitude" was Steve Jobs. What he did after a company fired him is an inspiration. Jobs didn't allow the firing stop him or distract him from bringing the vision he saw would change the world through his ideas and technology. His "winning attitude" caused him to be rehired and eventually become the CEO of that company. Just because others gave up on you does not mean that you should give up on your vision to manifest your reality.

You can win your win by not giving up on yourself
—Jekalyn Carr

Winning Attitude Produces Greatness

Another inspiration is Cathy Hughes, an extraordinary radio and television marketing visionary. Born in Omaha, Nebraska, she started her career at a station called KOWN. Later, she moved to Washington D.C. after accepting a job at Howard University. She went from being a lecturer to the general sales manager of that station to becoming the founder of Radio One. Her "winning attitude" of pursuing her vision has now earned her a net worth around $460 million. When her company went public in 1999, she became the first African-American woman to head a publicly traded corporation. Her positive and "winning attitude" helped bring success to her and her affiliates in the radio industry. Her accomplisments allowed her to take the industry further, by launching the network TV One, (now Urban One.) Her vision was not only on the radio anymore, but now it was touching lives through television.

I read in one of her interviews how she shared her vision to invest in a radio station for the first time and received a "No!"— the second time a "No!", the third time a "No!", until her 33rd time when she received her first "Yes!" After hearing no on the third time, many people would have given up and responded with, "This is not for me." Others would have begun to question and doubt their vision. Her passion for her vision took persistence in pursuing her first "Yes!"

People sometimes become bitter and misguided by contrary information. Even in the "No!" moments in your life, you must keep pushing forward until the "Yes!" flows in, one after the other. Your response to the "No!" is what changes it to "Yes!". Cathy Hughes is an example of a person having a "winning attitude" that produced greatness. A "No!" will only set you back, if you permit it to do so. What if she had accepted all the "No's"? It is easier to walk away and not push for what you believe, but the reward is more significant when you are persistent about bringing your vision to reality.

Never let a "No!" keep your great ideas bottled up in you.
—Jekalyn Carr

Daymond John, fashion and business mogul, known for the FUBU brand. He first began working out of his mother's basement making and selling hats, with high expectations of his vision coming true. As he was building his brand, he went from selling hats to becoming an author, television personality, investor, and the list keeps going. He went from seeking investments for his company to becoming a primary investor for others. It began with a thought, and he didn't allow the thought to sit in midair, but he learn how to bring it to actuality. He went to an individual that helped him with his first step, which was his mother. She deposited in him skills to sew.

You need to connect with people who will help push and pull the vision out of you. For Daymond to go from thought to where he is now, is related to the "winning attitude" he carried. He didn't allow the errors, the "No's," and brokenness prevent him from building a brand that is admired around the world. He isn't a person known only around the streets of New York, but now he is known to the world for choosing to have the right attitude.

Learning to Win

"Winning" can be a learned behavior. Not everyone will have the self-esteem to "win." Many people have different backgrounds that limit their understanding of what they possess. I learned to carry the right attitude about thinking confident to gain success in my life. If you are around people who are always bitter and grouchy, you will take on the same type of mentality. On the other hand, if you surround yourself with people full of joy who finds good things to say even in negativity, you will then learn to take on that "winning attitude."

When people respond under pressure with, "I quit!" or "I give up," it might be a reflection of the environment, attitudes, and words to which they are exposed. You may have to be the one who tells that individual "You can make it. I will stay here and watch you as you try." Give them another point of view. Allow them to learn from you and teach them to raise their hand to declare a victory. Inspiring others to" win" will help build their morale. Sometimes people need that extra push. Let's be clear, having a "winning attitude" does not mean you have all the answers and resources, but the 'winning attitude" is what gives you the desire to get the answers so that you can get the resources to win.

> *"Winning" people push others to "win."*
> *—Jekalyn Carr*

You may not always meet the expectations of others. You may not fit the profile or image others think is required to carry a "winning" title, but don't try to change what has been working for you to suit others. The techniques that others use may work well for them, but your methods may work better for you.

You may have read the Bible story about David, how he slayed Goliath, the Philistine giant. Despite David's small size in comparison to Goliath, despite hearing all the voices saying, "It's impossible," despite people laughing and thinking David was idiotic, David held on to his "winning attitude." He knew that his God was before him and God is greater than any negativity that was against him. David didn't run from the giant when he saw its dimension or muscular build. He said. "Who is this uncircumcised Philistine talking bad about my God." His "winning attitude" didn't let Goliath's size block his sight and vision of who he was.

When people are up against a giant in their lives, they begin to compare their sizes and look at the odds against them. David's "winning attitude" was bigger than the giant. You have to think victoriously over the things that may try to challenge the plans that God has for you. If David didn't have the right attitude, his people would have come under bondage to this giant. You must have the attitude that what you are doing will help others. David sized the giant up not by fear but by victory. People sometimes look at the problem more than they look at the authority and power that they have. They forgot that they are wonderfully made in the image of God. Looking at the dilemma brings on fear and puts people in a place of being intimidated by something that God has already given them victory over.

You have to do what David did. He reminded himself that God gave him victory to kill a bear and a lion. (1 Samuel 17:36 KJV) Thinking about his past successes gave him the push and strength to speak against this giant. David remembered the bear was bigger than him, so this third time should be a charm. Always remember the last two giants you had to face when a giant appears in your life. They are much bigger than you, but you will be victorious.

Audibly quote this scripture (2 Corinthians 2:14), *"Now thanks be unto God, which always causeth us to triumph in Christ, and maketh manifest the savour of his knowledge by us in every place."*

You must know what the word says you have the power to do. It causes you to triumph. So, when you look at your giant in your life, never look at it with the idea of being defeated, but see your triumph in this matter.

David saw the size of Goliath with his eyes, but the "winning attitude" in his heart would not let him focus on the outer appearance of the giant, but made him understand the champion inside of himself. David had a heart. It's not always the size that determines a win, but it's the heart, vision, and attitude. David had heart, which means he could stand up to adversity. 1 Samuel 17: 32 says, *"And David said to Saul, let no man's heart fail because of him; thy servant will go and fight with this Philistine."* *David told Saul not to let his heart fail.*

Your bravery to take on anything lies in your heart. With David's "winning attitude" of faith and belief, he slew the giant and everybody that doubted him stood in amazement. You will have people standing in awe of how God is using you to do things that seem impossible. Because you have the "winning attitude," you are going to slay the things that others could not.

David's oldest brother Eliab had heard what David said unto the men and became angry:

> *"... and he said, why camest thou down hither? and with whom hast thou left those few sheep in the wilderness? I know thy pride, and the naughtiness of thine heart; for thou art come down that thou mightest see the battle. And David said, "What have I now done? Is there not a cause?"*
> 1 Samuel 17:28-29 KJV

His brother was telling him, "You need to get back to watching the sheep — something that you can handle." Sometimes people will mistake your "winning attitude" of faith for pride, but don't allow them to talk you back down to something from which you have already graduated. Just because others attained a certain level and stopped, doesn't mean you should discontinue your elevation.

Eliab refers to David's heart to win as naughtiness, but what others see in you is not what God sees. Here is a clear example of how people can mistake the blessing that's in your life for something negative because they do not know your background. Eliab, Saul, and the others didn't realize that David had been in battle. What man thought should qualify you is not always what God says. David was trained for war by killing a bear and lion. The people in the armies were qualified through training and battles. Even though people haven't seen what you have been through, or you didn't go through what they went through, does not indicate you don't qualify for the promotion God gives. David didn't care if other people didn't have the heart or "winning attitude." Others scattered and hid so that they wouldn't have to go against Goliath. In life, you must face the giant to get your reward. If you don't confront the giant, you will miss your blessing. You have to say, "I am more than a conqueror."

Oh, by the way, David was rewarded for his "winning attitude." Get ready to experience the rewards coming into your life and house because you held on, even though the giant was 10 times your size or more. The bigger the problem looks, the bigger your winning attitude must be.

Your "winning attitude" may cause people to ridicule you in the beginning, but they will soon acknowledge your win, just as David's older brother had. He told David, "I couldn't believe you beat the giant. Nobody wanted to do it, but you made history for our family."

The Midianites outnumbered Gideon and his men. He went from having an army of 32,000 down to 300 (Judges 7:1-8 KJV) to go to war with the Midianites. Gideon activated his "winning attitude," and with the help of God, Israel won the victory. Jehosaphat! When his enemies came together as a force to defeat him and Israel, he activated his "winning attitude," and the force that is greater than any other force caused him to come through unscathed. We must remember there is no power greater than the power of God that is working for us. Right there in the midst of all impossibilities, according to man, activate your "winning attitude" and allow God to help you win!

An assured attitude carries a great deal of weight when pursuing something that you believe. If you take the approach that you will accomplish what you are going after, you have opened a gateway to achieve that goal. Your position is not determined by how much you know, but by what you believe that you can make happen.

Attitudes affect everyone who crosses your path. When you walk into a restaurant, and the hostess greets you with a smile, it makes you feel welcomed. If you walk into a restaurant and no one greets your party, you may perceive you're not so welcomed. The attitude of a smile brings a smile, and the manner of a frown brings a frown.

Realize that on your run to your victory, you may not know what you will encounter, but if you believe, you will be on the right path to executing the vision.

Countless things happen in life that can come to detour you from having a "winning attitude." Now what comes out of it is what you give into it. You must know how to handle yourself under pressure, even before something unconstructive happens. I found the best way to steer in the right direction, when dealing with negativity is not to give it a platform. Do not bring it into your space. Not accepting negativity into your space may be tough but the less attention you pay the negativity, the more you can give notice to the positive things in life. It's not wise to spend all your time clapping back (term used to say something back to someone that is perhaps angry at you or doesn't agree with you). You can't chase every lie. If you continue to give your time to the negative stuff, you will lose quality time to keep producing the great things in your life.

No one likes to hear negative things about themselves, but you need to put it in God's hand and let him get you vindication in the matter. Even if what people say about you is accurate, take the time and correct yourself. Ask God for forgiveness and get back into the race.

Don't let the failures stop you from winning. When you learn failures are a distraction to pull you away from your assignment, you should stop, drop and roll, which is the expression you hear from firefighters when your clothes catch on fire. You have to think that the fire you are under is on the outer surface. The outer surface is where you must protect the gifts that are on the inside of you. That's why you should stop, drop to your knees, pray and roll on. You must stay focused on finishing your race and the opportunity to help others. You may not be able to handle all the issues, but your God in heaven controls all things. When you are working on things that can make other people's lives and your life better, you don't have the time to give negativity an opportunity to obstruct your "winning attitude" and your vision.

Thinking to Win

Your thoughts should challenge you. If your thoughts don't challenge you, you will move forward in life without a purpose. When people's thoughts does not challenge them, great ideas and visions are masked. We must uncover the theories that have been lying dormant. Yes, we must unlock our mind's potential to excel.

Your thoughts should keep you asking, "What else can I do to bring *increase* to others and my life?" Knowing that we all have an opportunity to advance, in life with our thoughts and visions, allows us to reach our highest potential. You must understand when you are given work, God has other people in mind, but he uses you to give people access to their "win". I want to encourage you to release the "winning" thoughts that will allow "winning" outcomes for all that is attached to you. I want to share this with you so that you can see how important it is to release the greatness that is within you. What if the things that we get the opportunity to experience now had remained just thoughts for their inventors or creators?

Activating Winning Thoughts

God has given some of you visions. He has given you ideas or inventions, but if you choose to sit on visions before you know it, somebody will come along with the same plan and execute it. They begin to prosper through the idea that you had. All you can say is, "I thought about doing that."

The Wright brothers and Gustav Weisskopf or Gustav Whitehead (which is the same person) came to be the first to fly airplanes in the world. God didn't only have them in mind when He gave the vision. He had in mind generations to come. Look at all the people who benefit from the airplane — the military, businesses, scientists, tourists, families, and ministries. Jesus didn't have an aircraft, bus, train, or cab. He had to walk. I am paraphrasing this, but I believe God said, "I don't want my children to have to journey on their feet for such a long time, so I'll use the Henry Ford and Karl Benz to create the first car and others will follow. I'll use Richard Trevithick to create the first operational train."

God said, "I want my entire nations to be able to hear the Gospel one day." So, he used Guglielmo Marconi, George Carey, and Edwin Belin to create wireless telegraphy with sound and images. They created it by using wire, fiber optics, and radar, for television signals; others will follow to improve upon their work. "I'll use Nikola Tesla to create signals for radio. I'll use research to create the Internet so that all people could benefit from it." These inventions have touched just about every man and woman on this earth in some shape, form, or fashion. When you activate the winning thoughts that you have, it will make a difference in people's lives.

A great number of successful people you see did not always have the success or money they have now. The success they have today started with an idea. My family and I often talk about our thoughts and ideas. We didn't have the money then, but we had a vision. We learned how to act on the concept to thrive.

Your thoughts alone can and will bring increase to your house if you pursue them. Winning ideas that are worked create opportunities and growth for you in all aspects of your life. Don't let the lack of things and resources that you think you need stop you. You can't focus on what you don't have. Take it step by step.

When you don't have the finances to push yourselves, allow your thoughts to drive you. You must learn not to waste them. Your positive thoughts become valuable when you pursue them. Your ideas are going to bring right situations into your life that you weren't expecting.

When you see someone successful, you must also look beyond that and know their success was once only a thought or idea at one time. Tapping into their thoughts or ideas caused the successful to walk into the place of accomplishment that you now see in their life. Your winning thoughts are a few moments from bringing you such elation, bliss, and success in your life.

Say this, *"Activated thoughts bring things to life."*

The only difference between people who receive credit for their inventions and other people that do not is that the individuals who received credit pursued their thoughts. God doesn't give one person an idea. We are all created in the image of God. So, His ideas will proceed to the next person to birth them, if one doesn't act on the visions and be persistent in bringing them into existence. I believe God will raise up someone in their stead to bless His people.

So, when God gives you an assignment, it's not solely for you to be great, or for you to receive the blessings. The assignment is for His people to benefit from using it. You are the vessel he's using, but He had all His creation in mind along with you.

The mind steadily advances itself with information, technology, ideas, and visions, but you must release the information. When our thoughts advance, everything around us advance. The thoughts that were released have taken a home television from black and white to color, to HD, to smart, and now to curved TVs; you can only imagine what the next advancement for television will be.

In 6th century BC, when the Greek philosopher Anaximander drew a map of what was then, the known world, based on the information that he had. His winning thought provided some guidance on this earth. We now have maps of all kinds because of the thought he brought to life. Maps have progressed from markings on paper to computers, airplanes, portable G.P.S., vehicles, telephones, and any other media devices that we can access.

The "winning" thoughts you release allows you not to be sheltered in a box where you only see one way of doing things. Yes, you can always revert to the paper maps, but with options available, you can choose.

I want to share this "winning" thought about a man named Frederick McKinley Jones. One of his inventions was the refrigeration for trucks to maintain the food and other products they carry by keeping the food fresh. Before his invention, the only way to cool food was to keep it iced down. That would only last so long, especially if you were to go for a long distance or an unexpected change interrupted your plans. Frederick Jones thoughts revolutionized the trucking industry. Many of you have great ideas, but for some reason, you have not activated them. I want you to know there are no failures in trying. When you put forth the effort and it doesn't turn out well, there is no defeat. It's just your training to become better at activating your thoughts.

You are a winner with great ideas, for you, your family, business, job, church, and in all other facets of your life.

You must understand that not everyone's an inventor, but your winning thoughts can help your family go from poverty to having more than enough. Your thoughts can work for you and your environment and cause people to treat each other with much respect.

You will win!

7 Ways to Win
1. Define what your "win" looks like.
2. Define your happiness.
3. Expand your thought process.
4. Believe.
5. Understand what you can do to make your life and other people's lives better.
6. Activate your winning thoughts.
7. Ask God for the grace to "win."

Words That Win
God said, "*But he answered and said, It is written, Man shall not live by bread alone, but by every word that proceedeth out of the mouth of God.*" Matthew 4:4 KJV.

Words are so relevant to our lives that being able to eat all the food that we want, filling your stomach with meal after meal, is not enough for a man to live. The words that you speak will give you life. Food alone will not keep you happy in this world.

Your words play a significant role in your joy and success in life. How you apply your words help determine your outcomes. Your words are the foundation of your life.

Words are essential to building a life. We speak words. We write words and words give us direction, understanding, revelation, and define things for us. Words are the most advanced way we communicate with one another. We are acquainted with each other through words. Friendships and relationships start with words. Contracts and agreements are articulated with words. We share our emotions and feelings with words. We teach and educate with words. People all over the world use words to communicate. Words are the gateway to building, elevation, problem-solving, and living.

People respect a man or woman who uses words well. When people trust your word, it is a lasting relationship; trust goes further than money. Your words can bring value to you or take away from how people see you. Your words reflect your character. When you desire to be acquainted with a person, you can listen to the individual's words.

Words formed the earth, so words are potent. Words shape families. Words develop every aspect of our lives. Words motivate. Words bring joy.

Proverbs 16:24 KJV: *"Pleasant words are as an honeycomb, sweet to the soul, and health to the bones."*

Pleasant words make your life feel sweet and give peace to the soul. When a baby cries, you calm the baby down with soft and warm words. When you use the right words, it can turn the angriest man in this word into a calm, gentle "baby." Whenever there is a crisis, the first responders request someone who is intelligent and trained to use the right words to converse with the person in crisis. Having a qualified responder helps people in distress to come to a peaceful state of mind. The right words can move anxiety out of people's lives.

When I was much younger, we all traveled to a convention, where I witnessed a man having a nervous breakdown. The man was tossing things all over the place. He was in such a terrible state of mind, even when the people who cared for him came in to help, he was trying to toss them.

They called my Granddad and Dad to assist. When they came to the room, they stood there analyzing the situation. My Granddad walked over to the man and clutched his hands around his arms and held them down. He immediately began to whisper into the man's ear. As he was talking to the man, the words that my Granddad shared with him immediately brought a calming sensation to his spirit. Granddad spoke the right words which became as honey to his soul. To this day I am unsure what my Granddad spoke to him, but I do know, whatever he spoke into this man's life, it immensely shifted his attitude. He went from being aggravated to being a warm-spirited person. Seeing that firsthand showed me that words could bring peace in a matter, or words can stir up strife.

Your life is about how you use your words.

Words grow like seeds in the ground. They are seeds that grow inside of us. Kind words spoken in your life stimulate the greatness that's in you. It's not right to call people who have transgressed or err, by their mistake's name, but they should be called by their proper name: a strong woman, a man of vision, a woman of greatness, fantastic child. Call them the winner they are.

Words play a significant role in outcomes and victories. Words often express how you perceive yourself. I will go further in depth later in the book. We pick up words from everywhere— good words and not-so-good words, but you must root out the words that do not match your character or the person that you are working on becoming. Words can bring life to a situation, or words can give a negative feeling. It's like when someone says, "I see the glass as half full." When you hear half full, you are thinking positively. The glass is almost full. You have a positive feeling about the matter.

On the other hand, when saying it in an opposite way, "The glass is half empty," immediately you focus on the emptiness. You think, "I don't have enough." You relate it to emptiness you may have seen in your life.

Words affect our spirits. *"Death and life are in the power of the tongue: and they that love it shall eat the fruit thereof." Proverbs 18:21 (KJV).* The words that you speak will cause you to live and operate in a place where you were designed to be — with happiness, joy, good health, and abundance.

Now, if you choose to use the negative words, it will cause you to live in defeat, captivity, with strongholds, and low self-esteem. You must continue to use words for the outcomes that you want to eventuate in your life. You must be surrounded by the right messages, conversations, ideas, music, books, information, and people.

You can use words to speak yourself out of a situation or keep you bound in that place.

When you release the right words, that allows for unexplainable healing, financial growth, and improvement in your family's life. You may hear me say this a couple of times in my writing because words are critical to your win. When you see things happening you don't feel is profitable, you must not complain about the negative, but call out the good you want to behold. Studies show when you raise a child in an environment with positive and proper words, they respond better in life. When you continuously use negatives in conversations, it causes bitterness and withdrawal. Release words that will bring life and cause you to win.

Here is a place in my family's life where I saw words made a difference:

I remember when my dad would tell everyone, "I'm never going to buy the latest model car. I'll always wait until the second year when the new model is introduced, so they can first get all the kinks out." As long as my dad used those words and spoke that he would never buy a new model car, those words limited him from being able to own the latest model. One day, God spoke to him and said," Change your words." He said God told him, "You deserve the best. I created the best for you." He immediately changed his words and stated, "We are going to get the latest model car." The next vehicle we purchased was a brand-new model.

He changed his words, and his words changed the outcome. Instead of settling for used vehicles he chose a new car. What if he had not turned his words? He would not have bought the new car. Until your words line up with what you want to see, you will never see it come to pass. It starts with the thought, and then the words give it the power to form. It's time for you to have what you envisioned by releasing the right words over your life.

Repeat this:

"My words have power. I now speak with words that will cause my life to spiral upward. I use my words to bring down strongholds that have kept me locked out of my success. I use my words to speak myself into the place of joy. I release financial prosperity on my house. I shall live the good life that God ordained for me. I can do all things through Christ Jesus which strengthens me."

Vibration of Words

You can refer to words as a vibration on this earth that God has given us to push us toward a winning life. Someone did a study to see if plants will respond to words. They put plants in three greenhouses. In one greenhouse, they played insulting words around the plants. In another greenhouse, they didn't have any conversation going on, and in the last greenhouse, they played loving words of praise around the plants. The plants where nothing was said, good or bad, performed poorly. Both greenhouses with the positive and negative words performed well. However, I believe if the plants could talk, the plants that were in the house with the unpleasant words would probably come out saying negative words. They would probably be using expletives to get their points across. Why? Because they were a part of the negative environment. In the greenhouse with the positive words, I can imagine the plants saying, "I love you or thank you." They would utter words to encourage you.

You need to choose which communication you want in your life. Your environment affects you. People often respond to their environment. God wants to see the best come into your life, and this happens by surrounding yourself around people that are reputable with constructive conversation. Sometimes you can't change your environment right away, but you can change your words, and your words will change your setting.

Scientists refer to a positive reaction from the words released to the plants. Your voice and the words you use cause a sound vibration in the earth. What do you think will happen if you release positive words? What type of sound vibration will it cause in the heavens? What I'm trying to say is, if you as a man or woman speak to plants and cause them to grow, surely you can speak to that word that God has over your life. You can generate the heavens, the angels, and God himself to form that word.

You need to talk to that dream you are believing for, so it can grow.

We should be causing a good vibration on this earth. I want you to speak to that word of vision, word of faith, and word of your dreams. I want you to daily release the right words over your life, and this will cause a vibration of favor and release an atmosphere from the heavens for you to win. The magnificent vibration of your words, will shake things that are not right and cause them to align with favorable opportunities on this earth.

Repeat this:

"Words that have been released over my life to bring on healing, deliverance, wealth, happiness, success, and wholeness, be activated now in my life. I receive every word that brings me life, brings my family closer to you God, good health, wealth, peace, new ideas, business, dominion, justice, revelation beyond my abilities, and authority to operate through the kingdom, so that I can speak to situations and mountains and cause them to move." I won't sit by and let the word of God be idle over my life."

Using Words to Alter Your Future

No matter where you may find yourself in life, you must not allow where you are currently become your final destination. Often, if you think, "This is where I belong or I can't live out my dream," your vision then will be limited to that place. You must understand it's only temporary, it's not your permanent place. If you can imagine where you want to be in your mind, you can tap into your future, and your future will begin to transform you. Your thoughts are a weapon that you can use to override your current situation. Your positive thoughts destroy all the negativity that may be hanging in the atmosphere against you.

Sometimes when you hear people say they are sick because of what they feel in their bodies, their words cause their body to respond even more to the words that compare with sickness. They appear to get sicker, but immediately when they say, "I feel good." I'm not sick." those words and thoughts cancel out the sickness they were feeling.

Years ago, early in my ministry, my family were studying the Bible story of Prophet Isaiah, Isaiah 40:3 KJV, when he said, *"Prepare ye the way of the Lord."* The translation of this scripture for my family was; We should prepare ourselves in order to see the things we believe God for to come to pass.

Truthfully, if you inspected our current situation then, you would not have believed it would be so. We had no connections. No one in our circle or family had did it before. When my dad released the visions, we received masses of negativity that was spoken against the vision and plans. Our position then was nothing close to what he was saying, but, our thoughts embraced that word he spoke. The words God spoke in our life altered our future. Using the correct words in our life redefined the history of what we knew. The thoughts gave power to our beliefs.

You must have winning thoughts to grow and change your course. Your course in life can change immediately. I want you to know; you must win. Many people depend on you. Your thoughts should challenge you and not allow you to become complacent. Occupy your mind with good things so you can be positioned to see good things happen. Even though you may run into in a rough spot, it does not mean you've taken the wrong course. It's only activating you to think and imagine greater. Nahum 1:9 KJV says, *"What do ye imagine against the Lord?"* God wants you to imagine it so that he can take you to that place.

Daily Word Habits

We are what we repeatedly do. Excellence is an act of consistency. The only difference between who you are and who you want to be is what you repeatedly do. Constantly use words that will secure you a victory.

Personal Growth and Development:" *I want to be better than the me I was yesterday."*

Balancing Life

Incorporate all parts of your life, so that one side does not overlap all others and create an artificial balance. What I mean by artificial balance is that you will be able to continue in life doing your regular routines, but without the correct balance, sooner or later you will have friction in your life. For instance, if you work a great deal and don't take time to breathe or smell the roses, you will eventually find yourself overworked and stressed.

I remember watching my dad as he worked, worked, and worked, so much that he hardly had time to do anything with the family. Artificial balance causes an imbalance. Yes, you may be providing what's needed, but at what cost to your health, family, and peace? From my observance of other people, I understood early that in the midst of all the hard work, I must take time to smile, go on vacations, and relax. Taking a day or two from your usual routine can help you think clearly about how to be wiser at doing the work, without much stress.

I travel quite a bit singing, speaking, and attending events. I learned it was vital to create the time to go to the movies, go to games and do things that will bring the family closer and provide relaxation. A balanced life is like medicine; it helps cure health issues. Many medical problems come from stressing and overworking. In this life, you want to have another option to look forward to besides working.

Many people who are in the ministry work extremely hard, because ministry places significant demands on their life. Just like work, ministry has to be balanced with family, work, vacations, and movies. Winning visions take time to build. In the building process, everything is hands-on, until you can pass the work to others to help.

False balance makes you happy temporarily. You shouldn't work so much that you can't enjoy the reason you work which is to have a better life. On the other hand, you shouldn't have too much downtime and not enough work in your life. Too much downtime can cause idleness. When you become idle, you don't focus on the important things. People, jobs, families, and businesses can put a massive demand on our lives, and we understand that, but if you are not around to enjoy things, you realize the false balance is not worth it. It's not good for work to push you to illnesses. Every one of us have room for improvement, so if you find you're putting too much time in your task, changing your thoughts so that you can rebalance and live positively. Challenge yourself to win in all areas of your life. You must become aggressive about a balanced life, just as in anything else.

Balance helps improve family life, personal life, and work life. It promotes your health and brings happiness to your life. A balanced life also brings value to your life. You will be able to see where you can maneuver and be successful in several diverse areas at once. You must know that you weren't designed to become a slave to one area of your life. All areas of your life should work together to help generate your "winning attitude." Work, spend time with your family, go on trips, take a night to relax, and complete your school work to maintain your balance.

12 Habits for a Win

1. Start each day with a prayer.
2. Challenge yourself to work on your vision.
3. Let your thoughts be positive.
4. Release words that cancel negativity.
5. Align your words with the vision.
6. Live a balanced life.
7. Let your words transform atmospheres.
8. Keep a "winning attitude."

9. Speak the good things that you want to happen.
10. Release words that will bring life.
11. Let your words cause a good vibration.
12. Understand the effect your words have.

You must keep working on what you see. You must know when to take your vision from part-time to full time.

"Now faith is the substance of things hoped for, the evidence of things not seen."
Hebrews 11:1 KJV

PRINCIPLE II:
WINNING FAITH

Faith is essential to winning. Faith played a major role in our accomplishments and walk. Faith was essential for my dad to sacrifice a profession to work with his daughter full time to carry out building my career. People often asked my family, "Do you know what you are doing?" Truthfully, we didn't have all the answers to the questions, but we had faith. We held on to the word of God that was spoken over our lives to be the head and not the tail, above only and not beneath, lenders and not borrowers, and living as a chosen generation, close to our hearts.

"The Lord is my shepherd; I shall not want." Psalm 23:1 KJV. Those are words, we spoke daily. Those words helped us to embrace the new territory we were living in by faith. We have to conquer fear as we walk in the promises we envisioned in our lives.

Fear and insecurity have no value other than to make us remember to exercise faith.

"For God hath not given us the spirit of fear; but of power, and of love, and of a sound mind."2 Timothy 1:7 KJV

Faith Replaces Fear

I've heard people speak of praying about a situation and waiting for guidance from the Lord. While this is an authentic exercise of faith, it is also our obligation that we work in the midst of listening for direction from God. There are times God will speak, "stand still," but there are many times we choose to discontinue working or moving because of fear. Fear is one of the most catastrophic forces that comes to kill and destroy our prosperity. Fear paralyzes and defiles dreams, hopes, and even the vision God has for our lives.

Fear has hindered many people from walking forward and accessing great opportunities in this world. Fear pushes you away from what you want to happen. Fear causes you not to step forward. Fear works against you. It always finds a way to make you doubt. Fear will tell you all the reasons you can't do it and how you shouldn't believe in yourself when trying. Fear will cause you to say, "I will fail anyway, and there is no need to try again." Fear will make you come to a standstill in life while everything passes you. Fear will make you question yourself and not trust the word that was spoken into your life.

When Peter stepped out to walk on water, he had two options — to doubt that he could do it or trust the word that he could do it. (Matthew 14:29 KJV) The point is not that he began to sink later, but that he said, "I can do it," he departed the boat and walked on water.

You may not walk on water literally as Jesus or Peter did, but your water may consist of starting a business, forgiving yourself of your past, or bringing to life the invention you envisioned. Your water may also include writing a book. Individuals are fearful of different goals, but no matter what your fear is, sometimes you must stare it directly in the eyes while going for your goal. Fear is not your friend, but it is the enemy to all. The Bible says, "Fear not" 365 times. That's enough for every day in the year.

Fear is not of God, which also means it should not be a part of who you are or what you display. The key to winning is destroying fear and its sentiments with the word of God. He has given us the armor and armed us with the word from which to combat fear in our daily lives.

The most powerful weapon God has given us to fight fear is faith. Faith is what we need to cancel fear and the paralysis it causes in our lives. The exercise of faith means we can move forward with certainty in the direction God has called us. The exercise of faith eliminates the need for us to consider what is and isn't possible.

Whatever we give our time, energy, and thoughts to will manifest and multiply. I want you to win, so I choose to direct your time and energy toward faithfulness.

Sometimes in life, we encounter circumstances that will challenge or attack our faith. When embarking on new endeavors and working our vision, sometimes we tend to fear because we see all the *impossibles* before we notice the *possibles*. What I realize is that even in the midst of our fear, if we allow God, He will make our faith overrule our fear. We must understand that nothing is new to God. He saw our challenges long before we did, so God has already created a dynamic strength in us so we won't be defeated.

Application of Faith

God wants you to continue using and applying your faith and prayer no matter how wealthy or successful you are, or will become. He glories in knowing His children need Him. As a parent, no matter how old your children are or how successful they become, it's enjoyment when your child comes home to reminisce or converse. God loves when you speak to Him regarding things he has done and continued to do for you. Before God begin to open greater doors for us, I heard people say, why use faith when you have money to pay your light bill or car note. Through my experiences and study, I learned even if you have a billion dollars, God wants you to walk in faith.

It's not your money you should trust, but God. When having God, with or without money all bills are paid. I can speak from experience. Several times when my family and I prayed and believed God, miracles would happen.

For example, when paying our utility bill, the teller would say, "Your bill has no balance, it's paid in full. My mom would question whether they were looking at the right account, the teller would then confirm that it was our account. We would depart knowing our bill was due, but God supernaturally wiped out the debt, reducing the balance to zero. We had the money, but even in my youth I believed God was saying, "When I bless you with more and give your family an increase, still trust me." I've learned, even when God blesses us, we can't allow our faith to lie dormant.

So, when changes happen in your life, your faith will birth something new to keep you going. You won't need to continue stoking your faith like you're trying to start a fire because you haven't applied your faith in a while. Don't allow your faith to be like a car that sits so long the battery has died, and now having to charge the battery to get the car going again. You should be able to access your faith at any time.

In life when people get comfortable in their current situation, they sometimes quit activating their faith, because it feels as though they've reached a place where they feel they have it all under control. We never reach a place where we have it all handled. There are people with millions of dollars who are distressed, so it's not the money that keeps you, it's God carrying you. That place is where you need to call on Him to sustain you and continue to elevate you. God is waiting for His children to call on His name. Nobody wants to communicate with someone who calls them only when they are in need of something. Even though God is gracious and merciful toward us, He wants to hear your voice, even when you have everything you want and desire.

Take a moment to revisit your vision, gird up your loins, and go to work because you have "winning faith."

I can recall my family stepping out in faith and launching our business. My dad would have discussions with other business owners who stepped out in faith to run their businesses. He advised us to spend time with people who are positioned in the direction we are going. He stated when he began to speak to the inspiring individuals, his vision, God had given, began to leap inside him (The baby leaped when Mary spoke to her cousin Elizabeth.) You must communicate with individuals who are carrying the vision. If you are trying to advance or grow, you need to surround yourself with people who will pull the best out of you. If your vision is not leaping in you and their vision is not leaping around you, consider connecting *with others who will stir up the drive and push you to be successful.* It's time for you to leap into your destiny.

We are extremely thankful for things, such as bread and butter on our table, but you must also think beyond things. Think beyond your job, because that's not the only stream God has given you. With Him as the source, He has several rivers flowing for you to acquire. The rivers are flowing in you, access them. Sometimes you need a push, the right word, or empowerment to help you walk into your vision. What's in you can be activated and begin to leap to bring forth the greatness that has been bubbling inside you. Your idea never disappears. "That's why when an idea comes along that's similar to yours, your idea is then triggered and causes it to leap in you. You then become revitalized. When walking in your vision. Don't allow the lack of faith cause you to miss out on your lifetime of living the great life that was ordained for you from the beginning. Faith causes you to succeed and "win." It's time for you to "win" in your life by accessing faith today.

Stepping Out on Faith

I asked my dad to share this in his own words so that you can understand what it means to walk out in faith:

> I knew God was telling me in order for me to achieve the visions that I had, I would have to work with my daughter full time. I struggled with that idea because I was in a comfortable place. I had stability in my job. I began to have conversations with God, saying, "God, I have five mouths to feed." Coming off my job was hard. I knew what it was to be without, so I lived in fear of that.
>
> One day, the worry was on me so heavy I had to talk to someone. I went to see my cousin. He stated to me that only a couple of people had looked out for him in his life, including his dad and me. I began to tell him I was thinking of supporting Jekalyn's music career full time. He stated, "I didn't know you believed in your daughter so much....Look, man; you can do it. There are only two things that are going to happen when you step out and do this: either you are going to make it or fail, and if you fail, get up and do it again."
>
> Those words stayed with me, I took them and ran. I made up my mind that I would support Jekayln full time, I remember praying, "God, I've never been a beggar. I have never depended on the system so, God, I trust you." These words alone caused me to walk into a life that would bring on success.
>
> I began to carry work full time from home. I begin to walk in another level of faith for my family and me. I went from working on a job with a steady income to trusting the plans God had for my family and me. My

income had shrunken to one-fourth of what I was making. It didn't matter at that time. All I knew was that I had to trust God.

In the first seven to nine months after I left my job, I continued to tithe on everything that came in. My family and I had made up in our minds that, if we said, "We are trusting God," we were going to trust Him to the fullest with the little and with the much. We continued to tithe and give, and around the ninth month, something just broke for us. Doors began to open from every direction. God had exposed the works. Doors began to open because we chose to trust God and his plans that he had for our life. We saw God's hand at work.

God used Jekalyn to travel around the world preaching from the age of 13 to 15 years old before exposing her singing ministry as he did with her preaching. Two years after traveling the world, God moved on the music ministry that he had planted in my family. I remember God had me in a service when His spirit began to whisper a tune in my ear with the lyrics:

> *If it had not been for the shaking,*
> *I would have never been ready for the making.*
> *If it had not been for the beating,*
> *I would've never knew how anointed I would be*
> *If It had not been for the pressing,*
> *I wouldn't be able to walk into my destiny*
> *He's preparing me. He's preparing me for Greater.*
> *I feel a shaking in the spirit,*
> *I feel a beating in the spirit,*
> *I feel a pressing in the spirit,*
> *Preparing me for Greater.*

> *"Greater Is Coming"*
> *Copyright©2013*

At that moment, "Greater Is Coming" was birthed. It referred to the olive. The olive had to go through the shaking, beating and pressing for its oil to flow. In my family, I felt that we had gone through the shaking, beating and pressing in our life. With this, God allowed the oil (anointing) that was in our life to flow. The shaking of our life-changing immediately, the beating of being talked about, the pressing or pressure from losing income caused tears of joy, tears of anointing, tears of birthing, tears for "Greater." Because we trusted God, he gave this song for Jekalyn to minister, in which God used it to touch millions to understand that the shaking, beating and pressing that they were feeling was God getting them ready for "Greater" so their oil could flow.

This song resonated with so many homes, families, entrepreneurs, people who experienced loss, or whatever the issue was, they knew that

"Greater" was coming. I heard so many "Greater Is Coming" sermons and messages that sprung forth from this song. It was as if God had sent the refreshing wind to his people and blew on them.

Through Jekalyn ministering this song, we received many testimonies about people getting their visions back, healing from heart trouble, getting jobs, seeing their children with a better behavior, having family members released early from prison. This song ignited people's faith to expect "Greater." The anointing that God has put on Jekalyn was relevant and touched the people's hearts as she sang each time.

—*Allen Carr*

My dad believes in me so much that we would drive seventeen hours at a time to engagements, just stopping to get fuel and eat. People didn't know who I was at the time, so we had to drive everywhere at our own expense, sometimes just having enough to get there and back. Never did I see him complain, he was glad to take me across the world to let me see and experience the gifts that God gave me. It was this type of attitude that allowed me to be where I am today. (Winning Attitude)

Knowledge of Faith

The Bible in Hosea 4:6 KJV says, *"My people are destroyed for lack of knowledge."*

It's time for us as a people to walk in the knowledge that God wants us to walk in. Information is a powerful tool for accomplishing something that you want. God wants us to walk in the knowledge of faith so that we can acquire the promises. When you have knowledge about your faith, you will obtain more than you can imagine. I feel led to share this with you because I feel there is a release for your house. I'm tired of seeing people walking in the "Moses generation" of having a promise, but not receiving it.

I want your house to be blessed today; I want to see you walking in the "Joshua generation" of living in the promise. The only way we can cross into our promise is by knowing the word of God, the word of faith. When you know the word, you will have a victorious lifestyle.

Faith allows you to have what you are believing for, to come into existence in your life now.

"Now faith is the substance of things hoped for, the evidence of things not seen."
Hebrews 11:1 KJV

Behold, I will do a new thing; now it shall spring forth...."
Isiah 43:19 KJV

In God, He cuts out the normal process of doing things. When you look at both verses, it removes the future out of the equation and brings what you are believing for out of your future into your *now*. That's why you must believe now. Your faith activation gives you the opportunity to have the things you never had. God wants to take you places that your faith hasn't even been yet. God wants to elevate you to those areas. We must get your faith to that great place.

You may believe God for something that looks very big to you, but God wants you to have faith that's even bigger than that.

The Bible says we go from *"faith to faith"* and *"glory to glory."* (Romans 1:17 and 2 Corinthians 3:18)

You can 't stop at the mountain faith, but you must go for the universe faith, after you reach the universe faith, go for creation faith after that faith, ask God to give you faith as He has.

If you are believing God for a house, you may realize that according to the natural process you don't qualify. Your credit score is not there. You don't have the money in the bank. You don't meet the requirements. According to man, you would not get the mortgage. What I'm trying to get you to understand is that *faith* doesn't look at what you don't have. Faith doesn't look at what your circumstances may be currently. Faith doesn't look at your credit score.

Faith doesn't look at your bank account. *Faith* looks at your belief. You may have heard stories from other people about what they had to do to get what they wanted. It's good to have input and knowledge, but don't let information get in the way of your faith.

David was told that to slay the giant; he needed the weapons the soldiers took into battle. He needed a sword. He needed armor. His faith said," I hear you, and I see that, but I'm going to trust this thing that I have, called 'faith' to lead me. Give me some rocks and my slingshot." An unusual victory occurred here because he trusted the experience that God had given him and not what man said. Faith will lead you in an unusual way. Why? Truth be known, it is because most of us need an unusual blessing in our lives.

Faith Skips the Process

Jesus saith unto them, Fill the waterpots with water. And they filled them up to the brim.

And he saith unto them, Draw out now, and bear unto the governor of the feast. And they bare it.

When the ruler of the feast had tasted the water that was made wine, and knew not whence it was: (but the servants which drew the water knew;) the governor of the feast called the bridegroom,

And saith unto him, every man at the beginning doth set forth good wine; and when men have well drunk, then that which is worse: but thou hast kept the good wine until now.

John 2:7-10 KJV

I want you to see this. Jesus cut out the winery process. He had no grapes, just water in the pots. All theologians, professors, scientists, the people who are in the wine business, and everyone else would say to make wine; you need grapes. They would guarantee you that you can't do it without grapes.

But God went to a wedding, and when the guests were thirsty for more wine, He told the servants to put water in the pots. He took those same pots of water and began to pour. Somewhere in between the time, he had the water put into the pots, and at the time they poured, the liquid became wine. One ingredient was added that you don't see in the text. It was called *faith*. His *faith* caused the supernatural to happen.

You see when they poured, the best wine ever was made known. God put the supernatural in plain water and turned it into wine.

I'm talking about your faith. I'm talking to you because God wants to see your faith increased, so that he can put the supernatural on whatever issue you are dealing with and turn it in your favor. If you want to see something change immediately, put *faith* to work on it. When your *faith* catches on fire, then your *faith* will cause the things that you are thinking of to spring forth. Remember what I have told you about your words, now put *faith* in your words.

Another example of faith at work is in *1King 17: 11-15 KJV*

> *And as she was going to fetch it, he called to her, and said, bring me, I pray thee, a morsel of bread in thine hand.*
>
> *And she said, As the Lord thy God liveth, I have not a cake, but a handful of meal in a barrel, and a little oil in a cruse: and, behold, I am gathering two sticks, that I may go in and dress it for me and my son, that we may eat it, and die.*
>
> *And Elijah said unto her, Fear not; go and do as thou hast said: but make me thereof a little cake first, and bring it unto me, and after make for thee and for thy son.*
>
> *For thus saith the Lord God of Israel, the barrel of meal shall not waste, neither shall the cruse of oil fail, until the day that the Lord sendeth rain upon the earth.*
>
> *And she went and did according to the saying of Elijah: and she, and he, and her house did eat many days.*

When the woman took her last meal and gave it to the man of God, He took it and added the supernatural, causing her to have barrels of meal that never ran dry, and her oil never run out.

Under natural circumstances you would say that one meal (spelled out **MEAL,** referred to or known as one eating or the piece of bread given to the prophet), Naturally one piece of bread cannot cause a lifetime of meal (spelled out **MEAL,** referred to or known as in this case as flour, or cornmeal in a barrel). There is no way one meal can cause meal to flow continuously in a barrel. It's not even possible, for a meal to be made in a barrel. That's not genetically or physically correct.

The natural process to make meal or flour is to purchase wheat or corn seeds, grow them, pick and clean the produce, and then grind them. Scientists, theologians, doctors, and people who work in the meal or flour business would guarantee you that it's not possible. Faith defies the odds and brings forth miracles unimaginable to men.

When a person goes to a doctor who gives them a substandard report, and the person takes what the doctor told them and puts faith on it and returns to the doctor, the Dr. then says," I don't see what I found last time." God will do spiritual surgery without a knife.

Your words and faith cause things to line up on this earth for you. The elements come in place, for you. Let me remind you that when God has something for you, He's going to cut out the natural process completely to get your need to you.

Faith can guarantee you that you don't need all the ingredients and the normal process.

God is saying, "All I need is your *faith*, and I'm giving you the meal or flour, and it will have a continuous flow. I want you to understand that you have "Everything" in you, that causes poverty to discontinue in your family lineage. You have "Everything" in you, that will restore your health. You have "Everything" in you that will help you "win" the court case when facing the judge. The "Everything" I'm speaking of, is "The Name Jesus." Use your faith to "win."

Look at Isaac when he sowed ground that was not producing. Isaac's faith caused plants to grow and allowed him to reap a harvest.

"Then Isaac sowed in that land, and received in the same year an hundredfold: and the Lord blessed him." Genesis 26:12 KJV.

Scientists would say there is no way in this lifetime anything should be growing now. Scientists will tell you, "The ground is too hard. The ground is not fertile. The ground is too cold." As it did for Isaac, when you apply your faith, God is going to let plants grow in places that man would say would never be fertile.

All it takes is right there in the middle of all the "can't" (s) — "I can't do this. I can't have that" and in the middle of all the "ain't" (s) — "I ain't this, or I ain't got this and I ain't going to get it."— trust God's voice and at that moment when he speaks, sow your seeds.

At that moment when everything is working against you, and all the negativity is coming against you; in the devil's face, God is going to prosper you. When the man says that many of you, based on your current situation, can hang it up, this is the right opportunity for God to show you that He has you covered. What you are believing for guarantees your faith.

Understanding the Truth of Faith

Many people get to a place in life where they are tired of hearing the facts and not hearing the truth.

The truth is:

You must trust God more than the chair you sit in.

Let me tell you more about the truth, instead of the facts.

The truth is:

Before there were hospitals, there was Jesus.

He healed the 10 leprous men. (Luke 17:12-19)

The truth is:

Before there were the state-of-the-art wine-making facilities, there was Jesus.

He took water and turned it into wine. (John 2:1-11)

The truth is:

Before there were buffets at restaurants, there was Jesus.

He took two fish and five loaves of barley and made an

"all you can eat" buffet outside, without stoves, pots, pans, chefs, and waitresses. There probably is not one restaurant in this world that can serve over 5,000 people at one time. That's the supernatural working. (Matthew 14:13-21)

The truth is:

Before there was a bail bondsman, there was Jesus.

Paul and Silas prayed, and Jesus came and bailed them out by knocking the jail down. He was the first bail bondsman. (Acts 16:19-31)

The truth is:

Before you could borrow money from banks, there was Jesus. He put the money in the fish's mouth and told Peter to go fishing and get the money out of the fish's mouth. Matthew (17:24-26)

When you borrow money from the bank, you must pay it back. Peter didn't have to pay it back. What God wants to give you, you won't have to pay it back. You won't have to work for it. He's going to release it into your hands, because of your faith and belief in the supernatural. God wants you to trust him for healing when you can't make it to a hospital. God wants you to trust in him, even if you never get the right credit score to get the house you desire.

Where there is a will, there is a way. If you have the fight, and it's in God's will, he will make a way.

You deserve healing. You deserve that car. You deserve to flourish in your business. You deserve to see your family saved. You deserve to have the house no matter what your credit score is or how much income you may have. My God is the God of the supernatural, and he breaks all protocol just to get you what you deserve. All God is saying is, "Trust me."

Many people believe God for things they haven't received yet,

because they have been trusting the ways they know, trying to get the best credit score, get the best education, and yes, all that is fine.

But God says I want to perform the supernatural in your life.

Your child will be obedient. You will have what you request in faith. Everything that God wants to do in your life is plural.

Psalms 37:4 KJV says, "Delight thyself also in the Lord; and he shall give thee the desires of thine heart." "Desires" has an "s."

If you believe God for property, for money today, God told me to tell His people that He has made Himself known today in your home to release finances, healing, jobs, and homes. Faith, trusting, work, and, your words have set you up and made you ready to step out into entrepreneurship. For those of you who need healing today, I hear God saying that just because you are under His anointing, because you are believing, He's sending a healing angel in your life. Your faith has caught his attention. God has healed diabetes. God has healed cancer. God has healed your ailment. Receive it now and shout," I am healed!"

Don't you let the devil sit on your shoulder and whisper in your ear that it's not going to happen. You are running toward the finish line, but somehow the enemy eases up alongside you and tries to get in your mind so that you won't have faith to cross over the line. The voice of the enemy will point out everything negative, instead of telling you how far you've come. The devil comes to steal, kill, and destroy. He wants to steal your miracle from you. Every time you hear words that are the opposite of what you are believing for or your faith comes under attack, I want you to rebuke the enemy and get him away from your blessings through your words and worship. Quote scriptures, declare and believe in what you are saying. God is going to push you into a place where *favor* will even surround your name! Your name alone will allow doors to open in your favor. Your name alone is going to cause you to walk on uncharted territories.

Remember this; *you can't enter anywhere that your faith can't see.*

Faith will interrupt the negative plans that have been conceived to keep you from prospering.

Faith will cause a child that was born with a birth defect to be healed.

Applying *faith* helps improve your financial situation. Loans that may have been denied, by faith can be approved. A spirit has been released to attack the people of faith, but God has covered you with the blood. It's your time to live in the abundance of his word, through your faith.

7 Ways to Increase Your Faith

1. Apply faith no matter what your circumstances are.
2. Talk with people who causes your faith to leap.
3. Release words of faith.
4. Trust the word.
5. Replace fear with faith.
6. Activate your faith.
7. Know the truth about faith.

"For I know the thoughts that I think toward you, saith the Lord, thoughts of peace, and not of evil, to give you an expected end."
Jeremiah 29:11KJV

PRINCIPLE III:
STRUCTURES TO WIN

Having a plan or sense of direction on what you are trying to accomplish helps you to hit your target. Using techniques and strategies are great ways to manage the outcome of your vision. Often when you see people who have a plan in place, they tend to execute the goals more quickly than those without a plan.

There's a game that I play on my phone in which the intensity of each level is greater than the one before it! I found, to pass each level, you need to apply a different strategy. This happens on each level. The strategy from the previous level doesn't work for the next! This strategy doesn't pertain to a game, but this is what happens in life! To keep winning, you have to keep strategizing!

You must learn what it takes to conquer the next level. The new level will require you to learn a new strategy. You must learn what it takes to succeed. It's like receiving a job promotion. You received a promotion because you mastered the work that you were doing. Now, you have to master new skills and approaches to problems appropriate for where you are. Your promotions bring new tasks you have to accomplish. You must operate from a different view and adopt new strategies to succeed.

The foundation may remain the same, but the strategies will be different. In your next dimension, you must use the tools that are necessary for you to win at that level. Operating in the same place and trying to succeed on what you know is not what it takes when going to new levels, you will have to upgrade your mindset to where you are going.

When building a house, once you lay the concrete, you continue to the next step. You must add on to the foundation. You can't get new results if you try to lay concrete on every level. Once you have accomplished the level, bring in the material for the next level.

Think Success

Often when we set out to reach a goal, one of the first and practical ways to complete the assignment is to think of it as finished before it's done. When you think success, it's as if you have envisioned yourself at the place you want to be. Your thoughts are at the finish line, but you must rewind and go through the course to get there. If you don't think it, you won't see it.

Our thoughts set a milestone for us to accomplish our goals. Sometimes the only thing that pushes us is how we think of or perceive the matter. Thinking is directing your mind toward something. If you have your mind directed toward your goal, it will keep your focus in that direction. The direction of your thoughts can either cause you to be successful or not to reach the potential in you. You may not always know the magnitude of your potential, but you will find out as you go along. How do you find out? You keep putting one foot in front of the other, one foot in front of the other, one foot in front of the other, over and over again. With your vision of winning, your steps will follow the path and allow you to see the greatness at hand waiting for you to tap into.

Positive thoughts release positive energy into the atmosphere. Here's an example of how your day can be affected. You may say, "I woke up late, and I forgot to do something, so I know that I am going to have a bad day." The thoughts that you have released have made your day conform to a lower standard of what God have intended for it to be. Don't let one instance make you think that you are going to have an awful day. You must turn your thoughts to a positive light and watch the vibe that happens in your day. Remember words are a vibration of us and what we think and release. Shift your thinking process to a positive way. Positive thoughts will cause elevation in your life. Do not think of what you can't do, but remember if you can imagine greatness, it can happen. You must think yourself into your victory! *You will win!*

Focus

Stay focused so that doors can open for you. Distractions come in all shapes, forms, and fashions, but we must not let them detour us. Lack of focus can keep you from being successful in your assignment. When you read the story about Nehemiah building the wall, (Nehemiah 2 KJV) he came under all types of attacks to distract him. Nehemiah knew that his assignment was greater than coming down off the wall and dealing with negativity.

One of the first steps to staying focused is understanding that the assignment is greater than what you are dealing with at this moment in your life. If you break under pressure every time an issue occurs, you will never be able to achieve your goals.

Realistically, when you become wounded, disappointed, and facing a major attack, or feel as if you have failed, it could weaken us. In this weakened place, you must respond with the right actions. Every time you plan to go back to school or start your own business, distractions come out of nowhere, but its what's you do with the distraction that causes you to gain fulfillment in your life. Stay focused on your work.

Martin Cooper, an engineer for Motorola, demonstrated the cell phone in 1973. What if he had stopped at every distraction before creating a cell phone that works. Stopping to deal with everything that is said will block you from completing the greater work. Anytime you are working on situations that will help people; distractions will come along to stop you.

If you are in the process of writing a book, all of a sudden, your family and friends want to hang out, the baby starts crying, your job calls, or you have to cook. All these things will drive you lose focus if you allow them to. You must figure out how to make it work because some duties you cannot get around.

Yes, take care of your responsibilities, but don't forget about the things that you must work on that will better your life. Sacrifices will be necessary. Are you willing to reduce your daily tasks until you have completed your assignment? Your focus depends on the sacrifices you are eager to make to accomplish your mission.

I want to give you an example of how not to allow issues get in your way and shift your focus from your assignment. I want to refer to negativity causing you to lose focus.

My siblings and I would watch my dad use this product on the windshield called Rain-X. My brother asked him, "What do you use that for?" My dad replied, "You put this on the windshield when it's dry and clean so when you are driving, it will help repel rain and bugs. When the rain hits, it will roll down the windshield without you having to use the wiper blades."

When it rained, I remember watching the water roll down the windshield without the wipers on. This opened my eyes on how to handle words that don't belong in my life. I learned that the wiper blades didn't have to respond to the negative because it would allow the rain to roll down the windshield while the wipers stayed in their place.

So that you can understand, in this scenario, the rain and bugs are the negativity. The Rain-X I will call our prayers in this scenario. Prayer will strengthen you, whenever someone is talking negatively, let it roll down your back. Whenever you recieve a bad report, you should let it roll down your back. When your children are misbehaving, let it roll down your back. When things aren't going as you planned on the job, you must let all the negativity roll down your back. Just as the Rain-X allowed the wipers not to respond, you must be equipped so that you don't have to respond to negativity. Let it roll on.

You must understand that when you worry about people who criticize you, there are **7.5 billion** people in this world. If you have three to twenty people nagging you and tearing you down, don't acknowledge them. Look at all the other people in the world who aren't giving negativity, but reassurance. That small number of people doesn't even add up to 0.000001 percent of the population. So why worry about them?

You must not let your circumstances or experiences stop you from pursuing your vision. I'm reminded of Prophet Elijah.

He was expecting a sign that rain was on its way. He could have became discouraged and quit because he did not see what he was looking for. Still, he told Ahab to get up because he heard rain.

> *And Elijah said unto Ahab, get thee up, eat and drink; for there is a sound of abundance of rain.*
> *So Ahab went up to eat and to drink. And Elijah went up to the top of Carmel; and he cast himself down upon the earth, and put his face between his knees,*
> *And said to his servant, Go up now, look toward the sea. And he went up, and looked, and said, there is nothing. And he said, Go again seven times.*
> *And it came to pass at the seventh time, that he said, Behold, there ariseth a little cloud out of the sea, like a man's hand. And he said, go up, say unto Ahab, prepare thy chariot, and get thee down that the rain stop thee not.*
> *And it came to pass in the mean while, that the heaven was black with clouds and wind, and there was a great rain. And Ahab rode, and went to Jezreel.*
> *1 Kings 18:41-45 KJV*

In life, you may not see it or feel it, but you must speak the things that you want to see happen, even when the signs indicate the opposite. Continue to speak success. You speak, "Greater is coming. Something big is happening in my life. I'm not a failure. I'm going to win."

Elijah spoke said the word and continued with it. He went to steal away and placed his face between his knees. Sometimes you must step away and not look at the current circumstances, and look beyond your surroundings. You must create a space to imagine in, as Nahum did. 1:9KJVsays, "What *do ye imagine against the Lord? he will make an utter end...*"

All Elijah had to see was a little light in the darkness. Ahab drew near and said I see a small cloud like a man's hand. Sometimes all you need to do is grasp your vision and run; it could be the smallest things to give you the push that you need. Your victory is not dependent on how much you have, but on how you use what you have. Elijah believed what man would say is impossible happened by staying focused and not allowing his current situation to interfere. Focus opens doors, by faith, prayer, determination, believing, working, and not giving up on what you believe.

Ask Questions

You will face many obstacles when you are walking through new doors while feeling unsure of what to do. It's new territory, so it's OK to feel unease. You need to channel that unease. One of the ways that I learned to get over the unease was to ask questions. Be sure to ask questions to people who can give you the right answers. Think of yourself going on vacation to Disney World. Once you arrive, you look for employees to ask them, "Where is this building or what time is this show?" You ask the employees, instead of other tourists, because you feel the workers are knowledgeable and can give you the correct information. Most of the other guests are trying to figure things out, just like you. Therefore, you look for a person who has experience.

In my preparation for new recordings, I always wanted clarity of my parts, my role and the role of others involved. I would ask the producer whether the song is major or minor key. How many songs will I need for the album? Whenever we discovered an area that was not well defined, I would ask questions to make sure everyone had the same understanding.

Whatever you encounter, whether a new job, travel, business adventures, ministry, and so on, don't be shy to ask the questions that will advance you and prosper you in completing your task. One popular saying is that "The only dumb question is the one that you don't ask." Asking questions shows your eagerness to learn. Asking questions gets you closer to solving the problem or advancing you to the top. When you have the answers, you can't be misled or misguided. Never be afraid to ask, "Am I filling out this paper correctly? How many times do I need to paint this to make the colors blend?" When you are going into an agreement with someone, ask the questions that matter to you and that will address your concerns.

Watching my parents, I have noticed that they would always ask the hard questions first. My dad says, "Ask it in the beginning, and you won't have to ask it in the ending." He states that it's best to ask questions before you get too involved into any matter. I found that this solution saves you from being hard on yourself in the end while dealing with the particulars of any matter.

Visions

When you are working on your visions, you will have to determine what steps are needed to make it a reality. Now you must understand and work the process of bringing the vision to fruition.

Bring my vision into fruition has been effective for me as a young entrepreneur. Even if I don't have the steps, I begin to study the area and direction where God is taking me. For example, if I were to become a builder of houses, I would study information about houses. I would learn about the building codes. I would seek out understanding of the field. I would ask questions to the individuals who are in the business. I would learn about the different materials and systems like the plumbing and electrical work. I would learn about concrete and the foundation. I would study to know all the steps needed for the process. It's important that when time and opportunity meet, you are prepared.

In our family business, my parents always included their children in discussions. They did this so that we would learn the business for our protection. My mother and father said that we should have knowledge about the area we are going into to handle it proficiently and not have it mishandled by lack of knowledge or by someone else.

I found that many people see the vision, but don't prepare for what they are trying to accomplish. You can't jump out there and expect for it to fall in place. You must prepare yourself to win. Nothing just falls in your lap. You want to be in position, so when the person that you are sharing your vision with will be able to take the full details and run with it.

Habakkuk 2:2 KJV, says, *"Write the vision, and make it plain upon tables, that he may run that readeth it."*

So, when you begin to share your vision, understand your vision and the foundation of the vision. I want to encourage you to learn information that surrounds your vision. Learn information that matters and is relevant to what you are trying to accomplish. There's an old saying, "Why reinvent the wheel?" Learn what it takes to be successful in your craft so when the opportunity comes, you are prepared.

In business, you can't leave anything to the imagination or make assumptions. There are many reasons I say this, but here is one example. If you are working on a project with someone, please be up front on the communications. You don't want the other person saying, "I thought you meant this," or "I thought you meant that." This can turn a good relationship into an awkward one. To win, you need to express any area of doubt that you may have so that when you get to a certain area, you won't have conflict.

You must understand that everyone can't handle the broken pieces of vision. Some people are the kind who can only show the finished work. Walt Disney looked at land in California and swampland in Florida, and he had a great vision. Many people would have looked at the swampland and said, "Why are you buying that old swampland infested with insects and alligators? You are wasting your time." He saw a place where families could come and enjoy. He saw a place where children could come and smile. He saw the parents and adults being just as happy about being there. In what many passed over and over because they couldn't see any good in it, he saw greatness.

Can you imagine him trying to share his vision with everyone in the beginning: "I'm going to buy that swampland and develop it into a theme park?" I imagine that he could only share his vision with people who would believe and the vision of beautiful greatness even in a grassy, non-landscaped, muddy, bug, and alligator-infested area. Some of you had your visions talked down before you could start because you talked to the wrong people. I'm encouraging you to take that vision God has given and talk with people who will help you dream and tap into it. Not everyone will see the vision until it's finished.

Avoid Mediocrity

I believe that mediocrity comes to steal, kill and destroy. When something is mediocre, nothing is special about it. Nothing stands out to make it memorable. We can already rule mediocrity out of our DNA. The creator carefully crafted us. Our uniqueness alone makes us stellar. However, we can fall into the trap of mediocrity. Whether on our jobs or in our relationships, we can find ourselves giving less than our best.

In the fog of mediocrity, you can expect no wins. Winners recognize that the success is wrapped in maximum effort. This effort must be given at all times. When we feel weary, we must call on God to revitalize and renew us. Winners operate with high energy and vigor consistently. We have not been created with mediocre hands, nor mediocre spirits. Inside of each of us, a greatness destined for victory resides.

7 Ways to Avoid Mediocrity
1. Get in the presence of those who think outside the box.
2. Allow your goals to scare you.
3. Use time like it is money.
4. Throw fear away.
5. Exit the comfort zone.
6. Change something.
7. Stop waiting for approval.

Be Confident

Confidence is like a perfume or cologne. People can pick up the aroma of it. The aroma makes people either like it or not. If it's a great scent, people will always take notice. If the scent is not so good, it will not get the response and compliments you would prefer.

People listen and give more feedback when they are talking and dealing with a person who carries a demeanor of confidence. Confidence plays a major role in your everyday life when you are dealing with issues at hand. When people misunderstand you and criticize you, you must be confident enough not to stop to entertain every conversation. Your confidence is apart from you knowing who you are and acting out of boldness. When you walk in confidence, it helps you not to walk outside of what God has spoken over your life. Confidence allows you to rest in God's peace, knowing that where ever He has you and where ever He takes you, you will prosper there. Confidence prevents you from being shifted by people to something that you are not.

How do you find this confidence? You do so by negating all negative actions, negative words, and negative thoughts that go against the champion in you. Proverbs 3:26: *"For the LORD shall be thy confidence, and shall keep thy foot from being taken"* (caught in a trap.) You have to build yourself up on the word of God to have confidence in your personal life and the marketplace. You must cast down everything that has been spoken against you. Things will be thrown at you to attack your confidence, but you must allow them to go over, go around, and go beneath you. Sometimes you have to learn how to apply confidence. You sometimes need to be pushed to be able to walk with confidence. People's experiences in life affect their confidence and self-esteem. You must learn how to convert the not-so-good encounters that occur, to positive actions to help you live life better. God did not intend for you to live with low self-esteem nor for you to live sheltered on the inside. Confidence increases your joy and happiness. Confidence affects your faith. You need your confidence to have great faith in God. Confidence lets you trust His word.

8 Ways to Build Your Confidence to Win
1. Understand what the word (Bible) says about you.
2. Make sure that you have great self-esteem.
3. Watch and learn from others who possess confidence.
4. Do a self-check to see what's holding you back.
5. Deal with the experiences that have reduced your confidence.
6. Create positive atmospheres.
7. Connect with positive people.
8. Recite daily affirmations that speak into your life.

Understanding Your Greatness
I often tell people that "great" is not something that you become. Greatness is something that you are. You learn how to allow the greatness that is covered up by all this other stuff on the outside to shine. Greatness comes in all shapes, forms, and packages.

Many times we shelter our greatness with the things that are on the outer surface, but to reach your great points in life, you must dig deeper. On the surface, you can't find the diamond, but when you dig past the upper layer of the ground, diamonds shine. You uncover the hidden treasures that eyes have not seen, nor ears heard. You unravel the things that will make you win. Pull off the unforgiveness layer. Pull off the "I don't have all my desires." Pull off the mask of excuses, and allow the caterpillar that's been locked up in you to transform into the amazing butterfly.

You have destiny waiting for you. It's your time to meet destiny. Don't you miss out on your destiny another day. Peel off all the stuff that you have allowed to cover up your true walk in life. God didn't design life for you to go to work, come home in the evening, watch TV, and go to bed. You should be implementing something that will prosper your life, prosper your family, prosper your ideas, and prosper your health.

"Beloved, I wish above all things that thou mayest prosper and be in health, even as thy soul prospereth." John 1:2 KJV

My family had to realize that God wanted more out of us on this earth than our going to church, school, working, and coming home. He wants us to make a difference in life. In this difference, you will find a place for you coming to life. You are not a slave to work, paying bills, or living from pay check to paycheck. No, you are not a slave to tradition, to past failures, or to errors in your life. You are called to *win*. Don't take that away from you. You deserve to smile, no matter if you work in the government, healthcare, schools, law enforcement, daycare, food, retail, ministry, mining, plumbing, or any other occupation. Don't become a slave to your work, but learn how to work with enjoyment.

Don't allow yourselves to become competitive that you forget how to live in the abundance that God has given you. (God's word: "abundance.") It's good to want to win. However, if you get the trophy but lose your family and friends along the way, that is not a win. Winning is when you can get the trophy and still have your family and friends to support you with or without it because of your hard work.

Understand the essential things in life that make you feel accomplished. Even though, the feeling of being accomplished differs for individuals, just know that accomplishment is in you, and that you are going to prosper. Don't allow yourself to say that, this is all I know how to do, because if something interferes in your life and changes it, at that moment you have to learn something new, you would then prosper in that area. Believe that whatever you touch, God has orchestrated it to happen, and you will prosper in your life.

"Strengthened with all might, according to his glorious power,
unto all patience and longsuffering with joyfulness;"
Colossians 1:11 KJV

PRINCIPLE IV:
PATIENCE TO WIN

We're living in a fast-paced world where things are rapidly changing. Sometimes other people accomplishments give us an indication that it was overnight successes when truthfully; it could have been in process for years before we were aware of it. In other words, we always see the presentation and not the process.

Great things take time, and although we may want things our way at that moment, God's timing produces favor and longevity. In the waiting, God is making, shaping, and molding us so that He can sustain us. At His appointed time, He will manifest what He has spoken. To every great thing there is a process, and for every process, we need patience. Anything great can't be built over night. The longevity of a successful outcome depends on patience. Patience creates a perfect work. Applying patience develops the right character to have lasting success.

In this process, you will learn how to handle agitation and frustration. Patience prepares you for unseen things ahead. You will find that you were not ready for some of the things that you wanted to have earlier in life, or you thought that you should have. You would not have been prepared to receive them. God uses patience to work for you and not against you. I've heard many people say, "I wanted so many different things earlier in life, but I thank God, he didn't give them to me when I wanted. If I had received the items too soon, I would not have been able to enjoy them. I would have lost the items because I wasn't prepared to handle such a great blessing or opportunity."

Most of us can say at some point in our lives, "Thank you, God, for not giving me that when I asked for it." Patience creates the perfect work; God wants you to be able to handle what he pours out. God's has *greater* in store for you, so He sends patience to work on your behalf. When the time is right, He will give you more than enough. Each one of us has an appointed time.

I look at the different time zones that we have. God used that as an example for me in my life. In North America, we have four zones, Pacific, Mountain, Central, and Eastern. The Eastern zone is ahead of all the time zones. When the sun rises in the Eastern zone, the sun has not yet risen in the Central, Mountain or the Pacific time zone. When the sun rises in the Central zone, it has not risen in the Mountain or the Pacific time zones. By the time it gets to the Pacific, the sun has already risen in the other time zones.

At its appointed time in each time zone, the sun will rise. At your appointed time, your sun will rise. We can't force the sun in the Pacific zone to rise before the sun rises in the Eastern time zone. So, don't try to force something to happen too soon in your life. Be patient and wait. Each zone must wait for its appointed time. Each zone must have the patience to let the sun rise in its time. When the sun rises, it blesses everyone in that zone. When your sun rises, you will be blessed beyond your imagination because patience created a perfect work.

"For my thoughts are not your thoughts, neither are your
ways my ways, saith the Lord.
For as the heavens are higher than the earth, so are my ways higher
than your ways, and my thoughts than your thoughts."
Isaiah 55: 8-9 KJV

PRINCIPLE V:
WINNING PERCEPTION

Your understanding of who you are makes you a person who wins. Often, you don't understand who you are, and that's one of the reasons you see things not lining up with what you now see or have envisioned. Many times, people give up because they think their dream can't come true. They get tired of trying, become discouraged and even broken sometimes. Not knowing who you are can lead to frustration, because you are used to seeing yourself in your environment. It's vital that your perception comes in line with the way God sees you and is not limited by what you have seen or heard from others that don't fit into the vocabulary that God uses concerning you. The right perception will change your life completely. I want you to know the truth of who you are and what God calls you to do. Your failures and mistakes are not your names. They process you to understand that you can live even after them.

How God Sees You

God came from his throne, gave up his seat and living in a wealthy place, wrapped himself in the flesh and became poor so that you wouldn't have to be deprived.

It's kind of like the rich prince Eddie Murphy played in the movie "Coming to America." You remember that he was chasing after a woman, so he left his royal palace to become poor and live in the worst neighborhood. Just like that, but at a greater capacity, God left his wealthy place to come to earth to chase after you, so that you wouldn't be poor. God's promises is for us to prosper and inherit the gift of eternal life and live the life God wanted His children—sons, daughters, and heirs of the kingdom — to live.

Our thoughts do not allow us to visualize or think as God does. God thinks more highly of us than we think of ourselves. The enemy will have you thinking that you are not who God calls you. God thinks the world of you. You need to detox your thoughts and begin to ask God to reveal His thoughts to you so that you can think like Him.

Just as people detox to lose weight or clean the body from the buildup of toxins over time, You must detox the mind to remove all the negative thoughts that were built up — all the thoughts that do not mean you any good, those thoughts that speak the opposite of who you are. The way to be free is to see yourself in the mind-set of God. All the negative information that man has given you, all the things the enemy has said and told you that you couldn't be, and all the things the enemy said you couldn't have must be dealt away with. You need to flush out the things you have seen in your life because they can obstruct your vision of who you are. The mind detox opens you up so that you can hear and see what God is saying to you about your family, your business, your ministry or, your health.

Often, what we have heard blinds us, and we need to know who we are, according to the Lord.

God thinks so highly of you that he has left the earth here for you to inherit.

Look at these scriptures:

"His soul shall dwell at ease; and his seed shall inherit the earth."

Psalms 25:13KJV

"But the meek shall inherit the earth; and shall delight themselves in the abundance of peace."

Psalms 37:11KJV

"For such as be *blessed of him shall inherit the earth; and* they that be *cursed of him shall be cut off."*

Psalms 37:22KJV

"Blessed are *the meek: for they shall inherit the earth."*

Matthew 5:5 KJV

God tells you that you can have the land. You can live in joy. You can live in happiness. You are the lender and not the borrower. You are a chosen generation. You can pursue your promise of being a successful businessman or woman. That's God's word to us. When you hear or see the opposite of what God has told you, that's the devil trying to weigh you down with his spirits to keep you from believing.

Understand that you can have what God said you could have. Go get your family Go get your money. Go get your peace. Go get it! Go get it! Go get it! It's time for you to be on top where you belong and not scrounging at the bottom. Understand how the word God spoke over you is waiting for you to obtain it. The Lord has coming to you a great inheritance, and He has given you these words of inheritance. When God blesses you, no one can change that.

God said, "I know you messed up." I know your errors, but hear me loud and clear: My word does not change; what I have spoken over your life is eternal.

God is waiting for you to catch up with His word. The word that He has spoken is lingering over your head."

When you read the story about Mary Magdalene, you find how much more God cares about you than all the wrong things that you have done. No matter what you have done, it does not outweigh how God sees you.

"Now when Jesus was risen early the first day of the week, he appeared first to Mary Magdalene, out of whom he had cast seven devils."

Mark 16:9, KJV

"And certain women, which had been healed of evil spirits and infirmities, Mary called Magdalene, out of whom went seven devils,"

Luke 8:2, KJV

> And when she had thus said, she turned herself back, and saw Jesus standing, and knew not that it was Jesus.
>
> Jesus saith unto her, Woman, why weepest thou? whom seekest thou? She, supposing him to be the gardener, saith unto him, Sir, if thou have borne him hence, tell me where thou hast laid him, and I will take him away.
>
> Jesus saith unto her, Mary. She turned herself, and saith unto him, Rabboni; which is to say, Master.
>
> Jesus saith unto her, touch me not; for I am not yet ascended to my Father: but go to my brethren, and say unto them, I ascend unto my Father, and your Father; and [to] my God, and your God.
>
> Mary Magdalene came and told the disciples that she had seen the Lord, and [that] he had spoken these things unto her.
>
> John 20:14-18 KJV

Mary Magdalene was a woman who had many issues before Jesus healed her.

She had been possessed by seven evil spirits. It's interesting that God chose to reveal himself to the woman first after He rose from his grave, instead of the two men, the disciples Simon and Peter, who ran to the tomb. Mary Magdalene was not just any woman, but He revealed himself to a woman He cleansed from seven evil spirits. Just like that woman, you might have a past that some people would look at and say, "You're not qualified to see Jesus first."

I believe Jesus revealed himself to her to show *you* that He can take people with messed up lives, "issues," people who have been counted out and rejected, and still use them to complete great assignments. That was a major assignment that Jesus gave

Mary Magdalene to announce to the other people that He had risen. There is nothing in this world to which I can compare her assignment to. Can you imagine being in her shoes, based on her past, and God still chose her? When you tap into the truth, it brings on a cleansing, which brings you to repentance. When you are chosen, God will bring you back to the front of the line where you belong.

Look at Paul in his issue of murdering Christians. God stopped him while he was traveling on the Damascus road, and the spirit that was upon Paul had to go.

Just as he did with Paul, God found you in your issues, with messed up spirits, thoughts, and beliefs, but He saved you. You need to understand, that if God needs to interrupt your messed up life and save you because you are the chosen one, He will.

The Bible did not say which demons or evil spirits she had, but it stated she was possessed by seven. In the midst of her having seven unclean spirits and situated in her mess, God interrupted the plans of the enemy for this woman and healed her from all evil spirits. God chose to reveal himself first to Mary Magdalene so that you can know, that it doesn't matter what you have done or where you have been. When God cleanses you, He will use you to do great things.

The Bible says Jesus used Mary Magdalene to announce His resurrection. In other words, He took a woman from our point of view was "good for nothing" and turned her life around. He used this woman to make the announcement that He had risen. Your past mistakes do not take away your identity as the chosen one. You are the one who's going to announce, that you've had a life-changing experience with your deliverer.

God will deliver you from low self-esteem, depression, insecurity, and any other malfunction in your life. You're delivered from accepting what the enemy has to offer. Mary is an example of when God says, "Let my child go!" Everything that is attached to you that isn't supposed to be in your life, will let you go. Even after God has cleansed and delivered you, the enemy will send people and obstacles to try to hold your past over your head. Some people hold it over your head because they don't want to see you fulfilled life, but you must know that whom the Son has set free, is free indeed.

Repeat this:
"My past is my past, but my future shall be greater."

"So when they continued asking him, he lifted up himself, and said unto them, He that is without sin among you, let him first cast a stone at her."
John 8:7 KJV

PRINCIPLE VI:
FORGIVING TO WIN

Whether you forgive others or forgive yourself, forgiveness creates a right spirit and freedom to create a win. People hold on to things that others have done, or that they have done, and it limits them, so they cannot totally embrace a win. Holding on to the past can cause you to be bound by emotions, bitterness, and sickness without strength to move forward. (Anything that worries you, over a period it affects the health).

You must learn to let go of issues. You can't control whether the other person comes and asks you for forgiveness, but you can control whether you let it control your life. Forgiveness gives you freedom from letting the past control you. Freedom allows you to see and react clearly. It takes away the pressures that would typically stay bottled up in you and releases you from them. If you don't handle forgiveness right, it can cause negative vibes to overshadow the loving and caring person you are. Yes, unforgiving attitudes can make you feel you are a victim in your life. That's why it's not good to carry them from day to day and year to year. Don't be broken by carrying such attitudes throughout your life. Let it go so that you can live.

Forgive Others

Here is a clear example of forgiveness that Jesus showed a certain woman who was brought to Him because she was caught in the act of sin. (John 8:1-11) According to the law back then, she was to be stoned to death for it. While standing there among her accusers, Jesus stooped to the ground and began writing in the dirt. This confused everyone because His response wasn't what they expected. I believe Jesus responded this way because He knew His assignment was to redeem people like this woman, as well as you and me! After staying there for a while writing in the dirt and listening to the angry accusers, Jesus stood up and addressed them, "He that is without sin among you, let him first cast a stone at her." In other words, if one of you have *never* sinned before, you have permission to be the first to throw the stone to wound or kill her. Many of you have did some things in life that others have tried to hold over your head, but Jesus doesn't hold it over you. He forgave you! It doesn't matter to Jesus what you've done or where you've been; His blood cleanses all unrighteousness.

In the story, after Jesus addressed the woman's accusers, He stooped down again and began writing in the dirt, yet waiting for someone to throw the first stone. This gave her accusers something to think about. None of them were without sin. So, they had to turn and walk away, leaving her in the presence of her Redeemer.

At that moment with her, He didn't look at her or address what she had done or condemned her based on the accusations. Instead, He shared a moment of grace and love with her, which gave this woman a life-changing experience. Jesus didn't look at the sin. The fact that He took His time to deal with the situation with love can be a lesson to us all. If Jesus can forgive, then we should ask for the same forgiving heart toward others.

How many people have we wounded because of our quick response to other people's mishaps? Before condemning them for their sin, how many times have we *stopped* and thought about the times we have been forgiven for our sins? How many times have we reached out with the same grace and love Jesus showed us? In the same story, Jesus didn't condemn her, but He redeemed her so that condemnation would not hold her bound. No sin is greater than the other, and Jesus died for them all. Once a person repents and turns to Jesus, He sees their sincere heart of repentance, forgives them, and freed them for a fresh start. They can now begin living life the way *He* planned for them.

You have to receive forgiveness and remember always to show forgiveness to others, by the same grace that you want shown to you! Forgiveness is important to win! Forgiveness is God's grace and love at work. Let me reiterate; it does not matter where you have been or where you come from, the love of Jesus is the same.

Forgiving Yourself

Often, the wrong choices cause us to suffer consequences and leave us feeling guilty and embarrassed. But the thing is, once you are forgiven, God no longer remembers. However, the scars are left staring you right in the face. This is where condemnation tries to work, but this moment is a great opportunity for forgiving yourself to take place. Once God has forgiven you, He expects you to pick yourself up and carry on with the new life He's given you —a life of beauty, peace, joy, happiness, strength, and prosperity.

You can't allow the enemy to make you feel as though what you've done is too dirty for you to approach Jesus. The beautiful thing about Him is, He doesn't look at us the way man looks at us. Truthfully, when He sees us, He sees past what we've done and straight to who we are in Him!

Genesis 1:31says, *"And God saw everything that he had made, and, behold, it was very good."*

When God created man, He looked at himself and said, "It is good." The thing is, we may change, but how He feels about us stays the same, no matter the sin. God being so merciful does not give us excuses to sin. However, it assures us that we don't have to continue yielding to sin because of guilt, shame, and condemnation. You have just as much right to repent and return to the Father as anyone else does. After all, this is the reason He sent Christ into the earth. The sacrifice that He made for us by dying on the cross gives us permission to get it right and stay right!

Notice what He told the woman in John 8:11, "…Go, and sin no more." While others were trying to kill her for the sin committed, Jesus offered His love and healed her completely. He's the same way with us today. Others may want to destroy your name, character, and even future because of what you've done, but Jesus says, "Come to me! I want to free you and make you whole." Forgiveness is and always will be a crucial piece of our life.

I get many emails and inbox messages from people who say, "How can I move forward after I have fallen out of His will," and they walk around with their head hung low because of their past. I tell them, "God knows your past." I begin to encourage them and explain to them that their past shall let them go because God let it go.

You must understand that your past may say that you don't deserve it. Your past says you can't move on. Your past says you messed up, and your past makes you think that no one likes you. Your past says your future is a wreck, but I want you to know that *grace and mercy* said," I forgive you now, so now your future will be transformed to the greater person that you are."

Grace and *mercy* says you did wrong, but because you repented, nothing can be held over your head. There's no longer any condemnation. As I wrote about the lady the people wanted to stone, but Jesus got in the dirt for her. His heart and love He has for you will make God come into a low place and get you. Jesus got in the dirt where this lady was. No matter what mud hole you might find yourself in, if He has to get down in the dirt to get you, He will get in the dirt for you. This woman probably felt very dirty from all the acts that she committed, and even more when people addressed her and called her by what she had done, instead of saying you are a beautiful chosen woman of God.

He cares enough about you to forgive you and to make sure people can't hold issues over your head.

Can't you just see Jesus every time you did something that you weren't supposed to do? Every time you went somewhere you weren't supposed to go?

He said: "Let me come off my throne because I have to save my child.

I have to get dirty.

I have to go to the club. I have to go to the school.

I have to go to the party. I have to go to the house."

He came off of his throne of Glory to come and save you.

(Matthew 18:12) That's why even if He has to leave the ninety-nine because one strayed away, He will go and search for that one. He will cross the lowest valleys, mountains, and fields because you are as important to him as anyone else that He created.

"Therefore all things whatsoever ye would that men should do to you, do ye even so to them: for this is the law and the prophets."
Matthew 7:12 KJV

PRINCIPLE VII:
WINNING RESPECT

The best way to see success in your life is to learn how to give respect. It is not about whether you know more, or that you are better than others. Respect is knowing that no matter what role you operate in; you must treat everyone with respect. Respect means you may not always agree with people or their actions, but you still treat them right. When you see older people, respect them by guarding your language around them. When you pass a homeless person, never look at him or her as if he or she is not human. We must understand that it could have been a family member of yours in that position. We don't know what circumstances caused their life to turn that direction. His grace and mercy have kept us all. We all like it when people treat us with respect, no matter if you are the store clerk or the customer, whether you are the lender or the borrower, whether you are the boss or employee.

Often in life, we may feel mistreated and disrespected by others, whether from our family, co-workers, or others. It's important to keep in mind that every person is responsible for his or her actions and life! I've found that if you treat others the way you would like to be treated, even if they have shown you disrespect, people will see the goodness of your heart and favor that. I'm not saying you should allow people to walk over you and beat you up! I'm saying that you can be the bigger person and stand your ground of integrity. This is also a form of winning! Every battle in life isn't won with words. Some are won with our actions.

When you go to a game with someone, and you are for one team, and the other person is for the other team, it's OK to support your team. It's OK to shout for your team, but just because the other person is not rooting for your team does not give you the right to disrespect them. Don't get upset at the other person because the team you were supporting lost. You must learn how to deal with the loss, just as you dealt with the victory when your team wins.

During elections, people have the right to vote for who they want. Yes, you can try to persuade people why they should vote this way, and they may give you their opinion of why you should vote their way. At the end of the day, you should be able to vote for who you desire and remain to be the good neighbor, co-worker, or family member.

Why would a nation of people who love God, be so angry at one another, because of how they voted? If whatever you are working on causes you to treat people wrong, then you need to evaluate yourself. I would say just go vote for who you want and once you walk out of that booth, no matter if people are on the blue or red side, speak and smile because they are people. No matter who wins the White House, the governorship, mayoralty, city council seat, or judge seat, you still should know that God has the last say so and that you are victorious no matter what. It's what you define as a win.

Letting Things Go

Letting go of things or the past that tries to keep us from winning is important. Letting go of things is similar to and has ties with unforgiveness, as I have explained in prior chapters, the importance of forgiving.

I believe not letting things go because of what has happened in the past and not forgiving can create tension overtime; it brings discomfort to people's health and life. I'm not a doctor, but I have seen good people who can't let the past go. Eventually, it seemed to challenge their happiness and joy, which affected their health. Don't allow the past issues turn you from being the loving and caring person you are. Not being able to let things go affects your attitude toward people. It affects the way you handle things and the way you communicate. Situations may occur in life to suppress your vision and affect your judgment of things, but you must evaluate what's happening and look at how it has changed you overall. To win, you must let the hard stuff roll off you. I don't think anyone wants to live their whole life angry and bitter, so you must take the time to address what made you bitter and move on. Let it go so that you can smile again. Let it go so that you can be free.

Winning Habits

Winning habits comes about with winning thoughts, visions, and words. Winning practices are a form of discipline. They say it takes 21 days to break a bad habit. What will it take for you to have winning habits?

Never feel that you have arrived. Never get to a place in life where you think that you have accomplished it all. You must leave yourself open to feel that and know there is more in you that you haven't tapped into. You should celebrate your accomplishments and achievements because you deserve to appreciate where you have come from. Don't let your success cause you to be complacent.

In my daily life of achieving things, what helps keep me humble is that I know there is more to be done. I ask the question, "OK, God, you allowed me to do this. What do you want me to do next? We go from *faith to faith* and *glory to glory*. I learned not to walk around with my chest out, feeling that I have arrived, because I know I will have a new challenge.

When you look at Oprah Winfrey after all the success she has and the millions that she made on daytime television. She could have felt as though, "I have arrived." there's nothing more for me to accomplish." Instead, she went on to build schools. She started her own television network. Yes, you may have done great things, but there are more things you can do to help improve life for others. Because Oprah chosen to keep going, she has given jobs to many people, by creating the network and giving others hope by building a place for youth to be educated. The youth would not have had that opportunity if she had stopped at being the #1 talk show host on television.

To have winning habits, you must be the best you that you can be. Don't try to be a duplicate of anyone. When you try to walk in other people's shoes, you will never develop the characteristics that you need to succeed.

Purpose

Wake up and do what God has called you to do, and you will have a productive life. When people are working, but they don't like what they are doing, they complain and find every reason not to do the work. If you are doing something to get by, you probably are not going to give it your best. If you are working somewhere just to pay the bills, you will do only what's required. I want to encourage you to find something that you will enjoy doing, but always put a plan in action before you quit the job you have unless God speaks it, and now it is on God to fulfill your needs. Sometimes the job may not be the problem. Sometimes you need to bring balance to your equation. Getting involved with ministry, taking a day every so often to treat yourself, or taking time to do something that you enjoy doing will help.

Many people ask me, "How do you do it?" The two best answers that I can give that I am called to do what I do, and I enjoy what I am doing. When you like what you are doing, it doesn't feel like work. Singing and speaking is a part of me, and it allows me to be happy with what I do. By operating in the call that God has given me, I'm able to see what others may call work as my purpose.

People who are skilled in math, cooking, music, administration or anything else will do very well if they are working in a field they love. Mainly because when it's something they love, it brings out the best in them. Just like Sampson, all of us were born with purpose in our life. People carry a winning persona when they are operating in purpose. That's why we must challenge ourselves to go beyond what we are doing. Don't settle for just getting by. Keep pushing, keep believing, keep dreaming, keep learning, keep growing, and keep having faith.

Location

Winning is being in the right location so that things can work in your favor. A man wanted a new car and a job. He moved to a city to make a fresh start, but the things that he planned to do did not come together for him. After a month or two, he moved back home, and he immediately received a job offer. A few weeks later, someone gave him a car. By being in the right location, he received the job that he was looking for and a new car.

A pastor in Georgia shared his testimony that he needed a new sanctuary because his congregation had grown. While he was driving home one day, God told him to get off the main road of the route that he typically drives home and ride the back streets. Soon after he got off the road, he saw a vacant church building. He would have never seen it on his usual route. After he saw the location, he shared it with his team at church, and he went to his bank to try to get a loan to purchase the building. His bank told him that it would take a while to process the loan. He wanted to move forward immediately. So, as he was walking out of his bank, he saw another bank across the street, and he said, "I am going over to that bank tomorrow." The next day, he and his team went to the other bank. He began to talk to the banker about his vision and the property that he wanted to purchase. The banker said, "I'm the one who's handling that property." The banker at this particular assisted him and were able to get the loan approved in the time frame that the pastor wanted.

This process all started because of a location change. The pastor had to go to the right location to be able to see this building. Understand that location is important to your process of winning.

Lose the Weights

When you think about running track, horse racing, or any other sport that involves racing, you need the right gear to run properly. Runners can't have on heavy clothing or carry heavy items because it would slow them down. In life, you can't achieve your goals if you are weighed down with stuff that will hinder you. Weight represents anything that can affect your run, like your past, mindset, people, fear, unbelief, and so on. With these issues holding you down, the finish line will look far away. You should evaluate yourself and see whether the issues in your life are pushing you toward your victory or have they become part of your struggle. You must run weightless. You need to pull off the things that throw you off balance, and the elements that stop you from winning.

Every time you say, "I'm going to go after my degree," the negative thoughts or fear will have you questioning and doubting: "Why? What for? I don't have time to do that. I'm not going to finish; I might as well not start." These weights will pull your strength in a negative direction if you allow them. I encourage you to learn how to reject the things that try to hinder you from winning.

PRINCIPLE VIII:
WINNING IMAGE

What is a winning self-image and why does it matter?

The textbook definition of self-image is the idea one has of one's abilities, appearance, and personality. So, there you have it, three wonderful points to think about. Your ability, your appearance, and your personality. It's imperative to have a winning self-image because it gives us the strength and confidence to walk boldly in who you are.

First, let's review the part of the self-image definition that states these things are "one's conception of one's self and one's own identity, abilities, and worth." This leads me to one of the most important things about having a winning self-image. You have to believe in you! Your self-image has much to do with how you feel about you.

> *"Now when every maid's turn was come to go in to king Ahasuerus, after that she had been twelve months, according to the manner of the women, (for so were the days of their purifications accomplished, to wit, six months with oil of myrrh, and six months with sweet odours, and with other things for the purifying of the women;)"*
> *Esther 2:12 KJV*

Having a winning self-image reminds me of the story of Esther in the Bible and how she went through 12 months of preparation before going before the King. Esther engaged in a year-long process of renewal. No doubt she had time to reflect on who she was and what her purpose was. Just like some of you, I'm sure at first, she may have felt it was a vain process, but she was changing and becoming who she was created to be. Sure, Esther went through a physical beautification process. However, that beauty was a reflection of who she was on the inside. Queen Esther had a strong self-image and cared about others, by risking her own life for her people. Her winning self-image affected her and those around her.

I believe a winning self-image is joined with your self-worth. You have a winning self-image because you know you are a winner. It is so important that we love ourselves and that we understand that having a winning self-image will not only affect how we live, but it will also radiate out into our environment and influence others. Having a winning self-image is merely feeling like a winner from the inside out! You should be the person who lights up the room or makes others feel better if they are feeling gloom. Your presence alone should make the difference in someone's life.

Your self-esteem affects your self-image. The truth is, that if you have a weak opinion of yourself, it will be difficult to have high self-esteem or winning self-image. What's the difference between self-esteem and self-image? Your self-esteem is how you feel about you. Your self-image is how you see yourself.

Many people battle with low self-esteem. Some people have gone through things that have affected their self-esteem. You may have experienced lots of disappointments in life, and the experiences has left you dealing with low self-esteem and wondering if you're worthy of happiness. If you are battling this issue, never be afraid to seek help. Nothing is wrong with asking someone to walk with you on the path to healing. You can find ministers and counselors who are trained to help you overcome things that set you back or make you feel as if you're not important.

 You matter! You matter to the people who love you, and they want the best for you. Make getting better and healing your focus. I challenge you to take care of yourself and present yourself in the way you want people to perceive you. Remember this is your view of you. The world can be cruel. Unfortunately, people may judge us by our appearance alone, and that can be disappointing, so it's imperative that we start with loving ourselves from the inside out. You are already a winner! You were born, and that makes you relevant! The image you portray should reflect your feeling that you matter. You matter to your family, your community and those who look up to you for guidance and direction. A winning self-image says to others, "I am confident, and I care."

Your Winning Personality

What is a winning personality, and what does it have to do with your winning self-image? Your personality reflects the distinctive characteristics and qualities about you. You could dress well and look the part, but if your personality is not pleasant, it can ruin a winning self-image. You should always be the person who brings a winning self-image along with character that's reachable. What I mean by that is don't allow what has affected your life make you a bitter person. Everyone's intention is not to hurt you. Some people love you and will stand by your side to help you deal with any issues that arise in your life.

You should always be your authentic self. Let people love the real you. It's not right to try to be like someone else. Being authentic helps people receive you better, and people can appreciate you for who you are.

Yes, you will have to perk up and bring "winning attitudes" to carry your winning personality, but do not let it pull the realness of you off the table. Make sure you are putting your best foot forward, no matter the situation you are in. Life can sometimes be challenging, and we all make mistakes, but never forget you're a winner. Don't allow others keep you down about your past. You are forgiven, and no matter what, you are a winner!

A Winning Self-Image

My world today is different from the world in which my parents grew up. They didn't have social media, and the awesome technology we have today. They didn't have facebook or Instagram, and they didn't have to worry about being videoed or photographed at every moment and having the images shared on platforms seen by millions of people. The World Wide Web has given everyone a way to share opinions and basically say whatever they feel. However, it can also be a wonderful tool, if used correctly. We can still have a winning self-image if we are careful about how our lives are portrayed on social media platforms. Make sure that you think before you post.

Social media is not the enemy. Social media is a wonderful tool for families and friends to enjoy and share their lives with others. However, we must be careful how we use it and what image we portray. Have you checked your social media lately? Is your image a winning one? Sometimes we, the younger generation, can forget that everything we post or mention online will be there forever and may come back to haunt us.

A friend shared with me her story of how she was called to do a job at a certain organization. She agreed to be a part of the event and give her presentation. The administration team told her that they were glad to have her as part of the event. They said to her that, at first, they were not sure whether they wanted her to speak, so they watched her social media page for two months to read her posts before deciding to book her. She didn't have a clue that they had been watching her, but because she projected the right image online, she got an opportunity to present her work in front of many people. This story drives home the point that people are watching our social media lifestyle, and we must be careful how we present ourselves. We must maintain a "winning attitude" and image online. We should be using these social platforms to display our "winning attitude" and realize the power they have to spread joy. The image you project can determine the opportunities that come to you.

You are a winner, and you can do it!

If you need to work on your winning self-image, I will challenge you to work on the inside first. Make sure that you feel good and have healthy relationships in your life. Be authentic to yourself. Being you is the thing you do best. Do things that enrich your life and those around you. Remember, it all goes back to you and how you see yourself. Be careful that you don't give too much credit to how others see you or feel about you. Giving credit to how others see you is sometimes a trap that we can fall into. When you give the opinion of others space in your lives, it can stop you from feeling good about who you are and what you have accomplished. This "winning attitude" is all about you and how you think.

An excellent way to develop a "winning attitude" is to have a mentor in your life. Find someone who has been where you are going or want to go. Good mentors help you set goals, and they hold you accountable. It also feels good to know you have someone in your corner.

Resist the urge to compare and compete with those around you. This can sometimes be hard in the world of social media. Remember to focus on you and to realize how amazing you are. We all have assignments.

Having a winning image means negativity has no place in your life. Negativity will eat away at a "winning attitude." This includes any negative thoughts you may have about yourself or your situation. Negativity is a force that drains those connected to it. It will quickly make a winning mindset a losing one.

It's important that those who are pouring into you are positive people. Ask yourself, "Are the people I surround myself are they downers (people who make you feel bad or always have negative conversation about others)?" Do the people around you criticizes everything? Ask yourself, "When I'm around them, is it always a dragging environment?" If you've answered yes to any of the previous questions, you need to rethink your circle of influence.

No one is perfect, and part of having a winning self-image is to accept the fact that we all have shortcomings. These shortcomings don't cancel out the wonderful winner you are! You can embrace your challenges and use them to encourage others who may be struggling in the same areas you are.

Authenticity is key! It's hard to have a winning self-image if the image is not your true self. Make sure you constantly speak life affirmations for yourself. A simple statement is "I am a winner, and I have a winning self-image!"

A Winning Appearance

We must treat our appearance as an extension of ourselves. We must tend to our image in such a way that it is a statement about who we are. Dress in a manner that says you are a winner. People will try to define you by the way you dress.

What does your style say about you? Are you a laid-back person? Are you a diva? A winning appearance and style should be fun!

Style is distinct to each of us. What works for me, may not work for you. Just remember to remain true to who you are and be mindful that some style choices may project an image you may not want. If you feel uncomfortable in certain clothing or don't feel confident, don't feel obligated to put that item on. Clothes are to represent us, not cause us to feel uncomfortable. Your clothing choices set boundaries, and are sort of an introduction before the introduction. Yes, it does matter what we wear.

Your winning image should represent who you are and should be appropriate for your environment. It's your style, and it should speak volumes about you as a winner.

Dressing well makes us feel good, and that's all a part of a winning self-image. So, have fun with your style and personality, and your winning self-image will be reflected beyond your clothes, shoes or accessories.

Winning Abilities

We all have something that we do well. If you don't think you have found your winning ability just look to what you are passionate about. That is where you will find it. Every gift and talent we possess is important and necessary. Your skills won't be the same as someone else's. However, as long as you are using those skills to enrich lives, you're winning!

Using our talents and gifts in a powerful way is important. It says a lot about who we are and the image we portray. Always strive to learn and grow your abilities. Keep learning and honing your craft. Your skills are what makes you unique. More than likely there are people who already do what you do, but no one does it the way you do it. Never let someone else's talent intimidate you. You are a winner!

In conclusion, having a winning image is all about self-worth. If you need to improve your winning self-image, take your time to do so. Always be open to a productive change and learning. Self-reflection is major in having a "winning attitude." Be honest about things you need to change but embrace all of you as someone who matters. Don't be too hard on yourself. You will get there. A winning self-image must come from a good place. Once you understand how wonderfully you were created, you are halfway there. You were designed to win, and you will. If you know you're a winner, you will exude winning confidence. You are your best coach. Encourage yourself often, and your winning self-image will always be evident.

7 Ways to Improve Your Image.

1. Know who you are.
2. Love yourself.
3. Know that image is not about
   what's on the outside,
   but what's on the inside.
4. Be authentic
5. Do not compare yourself to others.
6. Know that your image is an introduction
   before the introduction.
7. Know that shortcomings don't cancel
   out the wonderful winner that you are

PRINCIPLE IX:
WINNING TIME

Using your time to produce great works, great conversation, and great ideas help set you up to gain victory. Monitor your time so that you can use it to work on things that will bring you joy and produce a harvest for you in times to come. You can never get back time, but you can see what you have done with your time. You don't want to be the one who says in your life, "I wish I would have continued to go after my visions, but I didn't believe in myself enough to pursue it."

You have an opportunity to be great and create greatness, so push yourself to walk in greatness. No one should be a workaholic, but you should see the fruit of your time to enjoy family, ideas, businesses, and other things. Most of all, I want you to understand that when you spend time with God, you are spending time with your vision. As you are spending time with Him, he reveals great works in you and great visions. In this time, He will give you the ability to handle and withstand the challenges that may try to come against the works that you are created to do. Whatever was supposed to work against you, He will use it to work for you.

I was reading my Bible one day, and I was getting revelation on how He created each one of us as a masterpiece. I immediately thought about Michelangelo who created such masterpieces. So, I begin to read and study Michelangelo. When I read his story, I understood that he spent time with God.

Time with God Is Time with Your Vision
The mind is a miracle, and many of you are walking around with miracles in your head. Figuring out mathematics: algebra, geometry, longitude, latitude, under-

standing science is a miracle to comprehend these things. When you look at building designs, creating designer shoes, purses, vehicles, and appliances. God put it in someone's mind to create something. Our minds are miracles that God has given us to create new miracles. There is something that God has placed in you that is designed for your purpose. You must tap into this place by reading, studying, researching, and spending time with God. Some of you are clothing designers, event planners, interior decorators, or writers, if you tap into your miracle, only you can do it as God has shown you.

I want to prophesy that God is going to have highly unusual things to happen in your life. Get ready because when God's hand is upon you, the unusual becomes the usual. You're going to get to a place in your life where you will start expecting the unusual to happen — unusual blessings to be released, unusual healing that the doctor can't explain, unusual ideas, unusual visions, unusual miracles in your household, unusual miracles taking place through you.

When you look at the artwork that Michelangelo did on the ceiling of the Sistine Chapel, you see that only he could paint it like that, because God showed him the design.

Michelangelo could have asked someone else to do it, but it would not have been the exact vision that he had. Michelangelo was so great that he was the first artist to have a biography published on him while he was alive. Michelangelo's father sent him to study grammar as a child, but he chose to copy paintings that he had seen in churches. When his father recognized his gift, he accepted that being an artist was what his son wanted. The father began to invest in his child. Michelangelo was smart in grammar, but his calling was painting. His gift was to create. That's why we must learn how to distinguish what we know how to do from what God calls us to do.

At the age of 13, Michelangelo became an apprentice to the painter Domenico Ghirlandaio. Michelangelo's father knew that he was ahead of his time, and he knew he was not just an average 13-year-old painter. Michelangelo's father negotiated with Domenico to pay his son as an artist.

As an artist, Michelangelo tapped into a place with God that created a miracle, and he painted something that revolutionized artwork. His painting on the ceiling of the Sistine Chapel depicts over 300 figures. The art is centered on nine biblical episodes, divided into three groups — God's creation of the earth, God's creation of humankind and humanity's fall from grace, and the state of humanity represented by Noah's family. The ceiling also has paintings of the creation of Adam, the creation of Eve, the Garden of Eden, the Great Flood, and the Prophet Isaiah. On the vaulting's supporting the dome are paintings of twelve men and women who prophesied the coming of Jesus.

Michelangelo didn't surprisingly pop up out of the blue and begin painting. His work started as a child and from there becoming an apprentice to one of the greatest artist at that time. Michelangelo was given jobs to paint and design. His work allowed him to be a sculptor and architect of many projects.

He received an invitation to Rome to build the Pope's tomb, and while he was there, he was commissioned to paint the ceiling. His experiences and preparation opened the door for him to have the opportunity to paint the Sistine Chapel. The life of Michelangelo proves that You can't sit, do nothing, and then expect doors to open. You must work until they open.

The architects Donato Bramante and Raphael convinced the pope to commission Michelangelo to paint the ceiling, but not because they thought his work was of high-quality or because he had a great deal of experience. They wanted him to compare unfavorably to his artistic rival Raphael. In other words, they recommended him because Raphael wanted to see Michelangelo fail so people would no longer compare their work. Raphael was known as a great painter until the word got out about Michelangelo.

God is getting ready to put the word out about the great things that He is going to use you to do. As long as you are doing nothing, and the enemy feels that he has kept you in your place, he won't mess with you until the word gets out about you. Then he will try to find ways to destroy you. Just as Michelangelo did, some of you will be recommended by people who want to see you fail. They recommend you or put you in the position, not because they think you are doing well, but because they want to watch you be ridiculed.

Michelangelo spent time with God, and what people don't know is that when you spend time with God, He will show the enemy himself. "I know you put my child here to fail, but I have the last say so in this matter." When people want to see you fail, it's not on you to try to prove a point, but it is on God. He will release you in such a way, that even your enemies will have to say, "You have outdone yourself on this one."

When people have wrong motives, they should be careful, because they must understand who is fighting for you. God looks out for his children. When you do research today, you'll see that many of the drawings Michelangelo created are used in the Bible and history books.

Time with God brings miracles to mind. The composer Ludwig van Beethoven was deaf, but the mind that God put in him allowed him to tap into a place with God to produce a miracle. He could hear and create music God had given him, and the music he did in the 1700s, still sells today, three centuries later. To this day people are still amazed by his work.

God wants to use you to create something that will make history; it will be a miracle for centuries. You are a miracle. The enemy wanted to destroy you as soon as he discovered that you were conceived in your mother's womb. You should have been destroyed by now, but time after time, God kept you. Miracle after miracle God has performed in your life, and He didn't stop there. He also put a miracle in you. He said let this mind that's in me, be in you. Once you open your vision to the miracle in you, He can then download your vision and outline the steps to produce the vision.

God wants to bring out of you the next greatest invention. Time with God is time with your vision. His mind is full of miracles, signs, and wonders. A miracle is an effect or an extraordinary event in the physical world that surpasses all known human or natural power and is ascribed to supernatural causes. Time with God causes you to step out of the natural power of this world and to step into the *supernatural* powers of God. By spending your time with God, you are getting ready to live your life in the *supernatural*. If you spend time with God, he's going to reveal the secrets of the heavens and the earth to you.

"And I will give thee the treasures of darkness and hidden riches of secret places, that thou mayest know that I, the Lord, which call thee by thy name, am the God of Israel."
Isaiah 45:3 KJV

Michelangelo was 13 when he started his work as an artist. That indicates you can be used no matter what age you are if you open your thoughts. Some of you have gifts that have been kept confined to you since you were a child. God wants you to unlock every gift that has been hiding on the inside of you.

He's going to use you to tap into treasures that have been lying dormant in you ever since you were a child. He said, "I will give," so not only will it be revealed to you, but it will be given to you in this season. He's going to reveal the hidden treasures, and many of those treasures are in you.

That's why you must spend time with God because everything that has been confined in you or from you, must be released. Your deliverance is going to be released because of the time you spend with God. You will be able to destroy generational curses because of your time with God. You will receive millionaire status because of your time with God. Don't miss walking into destiny because you didn't spend time with God. Your family's breakthrough is lying in the time you spend with God. He's going to give you something that will revolutionize your family. I just believe that if you tap into what he has for you, your success is going to come more quickly than you expected. You won't have to wait for six to ten years. The reason I know this to be true is that the same year I tapped into my gifts, God took me across the world.

I didn't expect it. If He did it for me, He can do *bigger* for you. You have a special gift that God has placed in you. You may be in a place where your circumstances are keeping you from operating in your gift. I know things may seem broken in your life, and you can't focus, but I want you to look back at Beethoven. He was deaf trying to write and play music. Beethoven didn't stop, but even in his circumstances, he birthed out music that is still being sold, performed, and studied.

In your brokenness, God is creating something in you. In your brokenness, God wants to use you to create something that will never die. I want you to know that in your brokenness, God is going to make you a history maker.

In your brokenness, God is going to birth the most awesome ministries out of you, if you're ready to tap into it.

Repeat this:
"I am going to release the miracles from my mind.
I have been holding them long enough.
It's time for me to release them.
Somebody depends on me.
My family depends on me.
My friends depend on me.
It's time for me to produce more miracles."

I'm not sure that you realize how valuable your time is. What I know for certain is that time is among our most precious resources. Time is one of the few resources that we have that we can't go back and get.

7 Ways to Make the Most of Your Time

1. Give yourself a timeline to complete a project.
2. Work on things that will create value for you.
3. Do not be idle.
4. Write the vision.
5. Learn about the area where you are working.
6. Spend time with loved ones.
7. Prepare yourself.

*The place where you are pl*anted you possess the ability to win. *Our family* was introduced to the right atmospheres and understood the value of words and the weight they carry. We changed the environment, surroundings, and outcomes in our life because we were used the right words.

Typically, when you have a conversation with people about their field, often they say this is not the right place for you to do this line of work, or your ideas don't work well here, but if you go to other places, it will work. You would hear people say that the atmosphere is not right and people's mindsets here aren't conducive to understanding the value of something. They may also say, "Everybody here has that crabs-in-a-barrel mentality."

I found that, sooner or later, after hearing the negative conversation over and over again, you will begin to take on that attitude as well. So many people told my family, "You can't do this here. You can't do it now. It's not the right climate here."

We learned that even though other people spoke those words, but we quickly understood we must not. We had to speak what we envisioned right where we were. My family thought, "What if God never moves us from this place? Are we going to walk around and say we're unable to fulfill our desires because of our current position?" That wasn't an option.

So, we had to learn how to prosper when many would say it's not the right season, time, or ground. We had to change our words to say, "We are going to prosper here. We are going to be successful in this area." Our faith had to be like Isaac's as he sowed where others said he could not prosper. You can't let others' experiences alter your future and your vision.

Every time we heard words that would place doubt in our minds, we would quote affirmations that would counteract those words. If we had to quote that affirmation for seven days, seven weeks, or seven months, we would keep speaking it until things began to line up to our belief. You can't fight battles with negative words and bad attitudes, but you must have the attitude in which you say, "I know what happened before. I know that others haven't done it, but don't tell me I can't do it."

You must know that greater is He that is in you than in the world. You can do all things. You can prosper in a dry area. When all you hear over and over is what you can't do and what hasn't been done, you must take on the attitude that you will make the difference. You will create faith in others. We need to see someone who can challenge the negative words with positive words.

You may know people who have tried before you, and their saying, "Don't waste your time." Yet, maybe you have a small still small voice in you that says you can. When you tap into what can change the negative outcomes, you can be the light for which others have been longing.

In prior chapters I mentioned about the visionary Cathy Hughes, who had to challenge all the negativity that people implied that her idea for a radio station was not a great idea and asked why was she wasting her time. "This won't work for you." I can imagine that she heard story after story of why it would not prosper. "You don't have enough resources. This is not the market or the city." However, she chose to go against all the negative words and learn how to prosper right where she was. She believed in her vision and applied herself to achieve it as others stood by thinking that this probably was not a good idea. She still kept planting, and now she has become a mogul in media across the board.

I can remember several years ago when the economy was terrible. If you didn't know anything about the economy at that time, you soon learned. All you heard were conversations about how bad the economy was and how it severely affected people. Many people suffered significant losses, and many families, businesses, and ministries faced challenging times. People had to adjust to having less income and restructure their lives. It was sad to see.

Even though all this, people still held on to their faith. They did not know sometimes how they were going to get by, but they kept good spirits in a low place. When people choose not to quit or give up, eventually things come back around for them. Yes, there was a lot of negative conversation, but most decided to learn how to prosper in a bad economic situation. People may have had to work harder and change some things in their lives, but they chose not to let their surroundings defeat them. They took on the attitude, "This is not my permanent place." This showed a side of people, who can change outcomes. Even though they felt the vibration from the negativity, and it shocked them, they didn't let it break them. Through their actions, people said, "I may have to adjust, but I am not going to let the economy take my joy." They chose to have a "winning attitude," which led them to prosper in a bad economy.

When hurricane Katrina scattered thousands of people, it was devastating for many. It shifted many people's lifestyles. They relocated. They lost a large number of items. I talked with a lady who had been in the middle of it all. She lost everything, and had to move to another city and live with family and friends. It seemed as if her life was done. Before Katrina, she had worked, planned out her life, and stayed on track to achieving her goals. This woman, in spite of all of this, she didn't lose her hope. Even though this big giant stood before her, she challenged the giant. She spoke, "It was just stuff. I can get those things again." When you look at it from that point of view, you see that she lost her things, but she didn't lose her life. She can gain those items again. She took on the approach, "I'm still going to prosper after all this is said and done."

I believe because of faith, words, and attitude even in tough times; she made a great come back in her life. Now, she's happily married, has a better job and can do things that she couldn't do before.

You may have obstacles in your life, but don't let them affect the winner in you. Your attitude, faith, prayer life, works, and fighting spirit within you have to be stronger than the circumstances presented. You were not created to be a failure. You may have trial and error, but never are you a failure. You were not created to quit. You may get weak and sometimes pressured by life, but you are not a quitter.

At some point, all of us in our lives need the right words, the push, a hand to hold, prayer, and strength to help us. Connect with people who will look beyond your circumstances and tell you that you can make it. Be careful of the people you communicate with. Some people make your problem seem worse. You can't talk with people who say, "Oh, this is so bad!" You need to communicate with people who will say, "This will get better!"

You need someone who will speak to that champion in you. People can be an asset in your life if they are encouraging you to be better. Unite with people who will celebrate with you and push you, and not give you reasons for why you can't pursue your vision. If you don't have anyone in your circle to push you, you must learn how to push yourself. Don't complain about what's not happening right in your life, look around. Most of the time, you will realize that you are in better shape than others.

Everyone don't share with you what they are dealing with or have been through with, but that does not mean others have not had the same or a similar experience to yours. They just don't allow it show on the outside.

My dad shared a story with me one time about his cousin. Whatever situation his cousin was dealing with you would never know it, my dad said. His cousin didn't walk around looking all beat up, hair not done, or clothes not ironed when he had problems. Dad said he kept a good, clean look. From watching his cousin, my father learned not to let anything take the beauty out of life. Carry yourself like the beautiful and wonderful person that you are and don't let life's challenges steal the glow and smile that you carry.

"And the angel of the Lord appeared unto the woman, and said unto her, Behold now,
thou art barren, and bearest not: but thou shalt conceive, and bear a son.
Now therefore beware, I pray thee, and drink not wine nor strong drink,
and eat not any unclean thing:
For, lo, thou shalt conceive, and bear a son; and no razor shall come on his head: for
the child shall be a Nazarite unto God from the womb: and he shall begin to deliver
Israel out of the hand of the Philistines."
Judges 13:3-5 KJV

PRINCIPLE X:
PROTECTING YOUR GIFTS TO WIN

We all have gifts, and we must protect them. If not handled right, they will be damaged like broken glass.

Before Sampson was born, his assignment was already placed over his life

Before you were born, God placed an assignment upon your life. Some of you were created to deliver your family. Some of you were assigned to the nations, and what the enemy wants to do is kill what you were created for, because he knows that you were created to stop his plans. As you are working in God's plan, the enemy may try to work against you, but he won't touch you. When you feel the attacks of the enemy, he is trying to prevent you from walking in your blessed places, and he is attacking you to try to stop you from receiving everything you are due.

The enemy wants it to look as if you won't be what you were created to be.

He wants to make it look as if you are not "somebody." He wants it to look as though nothing good is going to happen in your life. He wants you to look like someone that you are not.

Whenever you see the attempts and attacks are making you feel the opposite of who and what you are, at those moments, you must speak against the plots and plans of the enemy. Use the word "declarations" — declare who you really are. I am the head and not the tail. I am blessed in the city and blessed in the field. Come against all the negativity with the word. By doing this, you will defeat the evil works and the enemies who do not want to see you prosper. Take your atmosphere back and release what you want to see happen. Let the devil know that he is a liar.

The angel of the Lord appeared unto Sampson's parents and gave instructions that no razor would be used on his head. His mother and father had to hear God for him because as a child, he was not able to understand the mandate that was over his life. He had to be taught why he couldn't carry out like others to protect his gift. So, with his parents hearing God *for* him, he could walk in much power and strength, and he could do things easily. He could beat anyone. As long as he was focused, he could not be defeated.

So, the enemy knows that if you stay focused, you will not face too many obstacles that you can't overcome. So, he tries to send distractions to take your mind from being obedient, being saved, living right, being good at school, keeping your body pure, and keeping positive people around you. He tries to keep you from being a great leader.

I want you to re-emphasize that the reason you can't do what others do is that you must protect your anointing. Sampson's parents had to tell him, "You can't cut your hair."

I'm going to paraphrase; I believe that as a child, Sampson was probably saying, "Tommy got his haircut. James got his haircut. Derek got his haircut. Josh got his haircut. Richard got his cut. Why can't I get my haircut?"

His parents probably told him, "The reason you can't get your haircut is that you have such an anointing that you can't afford to jeopardize or lose."

If you want to be great in life, be all you can be, as the Army says, you must make sacrifices to protect your gifts. No, you can't run with everyone. You can't say everything that you hear. You can't watch everything on TV. You can't listen to all kinds of music. You must separate yourself. Because of the glory that's upon you and that you carry, you can't let anything interfere with it.

As a youth, it's imperitve that you know who is hearing God for you. Your mother, your father, and your pastor are in your life to teach you proper values. Their job is to teach you about the good and the bad in life. They are to protect you from the issues that would try to lure you onto the wrong path. They teach you about what will happen if you go against your purpose. It is very important that we have leaders in our life because they train us to make our ears more sensitive to hear and decipher the good from the bad.

When your leaders inform you that it is not wise to be a part of a crowd that's, take heed. They're informing you because he or she sees something greater in you and is trying to protect the purpose that's upon your life. (It's not always expedient to do things, because you are of age, because some things will attack your character)

When your leader tells you to wait a few months before step out, they are only trying to protect you so that you wouldn't have regrets. Your leader knows that if you get out there too soon, people will criticize you and make you crawl up into a shell and say, "I'm not going out anymore." With Sampson's parents obeying and protecting him, he could deliver Israel out of the hands of the Philistines.

It was not just upon Sampson to obey, but it was also for his parents to obey. Parents, that's why when God speaks to you about your child's actions, it's very important to obey, even if everyone else is allowing their children do it. He's trying to protect the calling that's upon your child. Sampson's parents heard the word from God, and his mother didn't drink wine or allow the razor to touch his head, as the angel instructed, because they were protecting his calling of being a deliverer. So, to Sampson's parents, it didn't matter what the other children did. No matter what other children are wearing or doing. Parents, you must protect your child's calling.

As a young person involved in work with other young people, I would share this in my messages to youth groups as I travel. You may not always like it when your parents tell you what you can and can't do, but they have been where you are now. They don't want to see you make the same mistakes they did. They don't want you to have all the bad experiences they had, so be thankful that your parents are trying to protect you.

Through the obedience of his parents, Sampson walked in his calling of being a deliverer. Young people, through the obedience of your parents to God, and your obedience to them, you can step into greatness. The devil presents peer pressure, suicidal thoughts, and confusion because he is out to attack the greatness that lies in you. He's fighting you because he doesn't want you to be on top, but rather, live in a place of hurt and pain.

Obedience of Jesus

When Jesus' parents were on their way home from Jerusalem for the feast of the Passover, they found He was not with them. They went back to look for Him and found Him in the temple.

His mother told Him they had been looking for Him and He must come with them.

Even though He was King, bread of life, the Great I Am, Alpha and Omega, Savior, Lord, Jehovah Jireh, He still obeyed his parents! He could have said, "I'm God. I'm the savior of the earth, creator of all things," but he was obedient to his parents and left with them.

By doing that, he found favor with God and man.

"And he went down with them, and came to Nazareth, and was subject unto them: but his mother kept all these sayings in her heart. And Jesus increased in wisdom and stature, and in favour with God and man."

Luke 2:51-52 KJV

I believe Jesus obeyed to be an example so that children of all ages can see no matter how old you are, whether the child is 11 years old or 21years old, you still have to follow the order of obedience. No matter how much more you know than your parents, no matter how well you can work the computer, no matter how much better you can read, or count, you must obey. Even as a child, Jesus set standards for obedience. The enemy is fighting against the spirit of obedience. He knows that obedience gives favor with God. He knows if he can keep the people from walking in obedience, they will not be able to walk fully into purpose. See, the enemy is after your walk with God. He's after your relationship with God. He's after your time with God, because if he can keep you away from God, he will try to steal your dreams, your vision, your purpose, and your destiny.

A shift will take place in your life, a shift for the better. A door will open for you to shift toward your greatness. This shifting will change your future. Some of you will find that the enemy has already planned to destroy you, but I'm praying now that this shifting is interrupting the plans of the enemy.

Friends, family, coworkers, and bosses will not understand or recognize the shift When it hits your life, they won't see you as who you are now. They will see you as you used to be, talk to you the way they have always talked to you, do things around you that they have always done. They will say, "Didn't we just hang out yesterday? You live in the same neighborhood as I do. You work the same job and make the same amount of money they make. You go to the same school that they do. What makes you more than me?"

It's not that you are more than them, but it's that you now see your purpose.

Your aim now is to pursue your destiny, instead of pursuing the things you used to pursue that weren't related to your destiny. You decide that you don't want to settle anymore. Instead of saying, "I'm going to be broke, you say, "'I'm going to work to come out of this place." The shift will have you saying, "I know that I work here now, but that does not mean I will be here forever." You begin saying, "I know I have done wrong and messed up in my past, but I'm not going to let my past hold me back anymore." Your past is your past, but your future will be *greater*.

Some people won't see the shift. They say, "OH, that's Carolyn's son, Derrick's daughter. That's James, Tamika, Chasity." They still see the old you on the outside, but they don't see what's bubbling up new on the inside.

After Jesus had been teaching and preaching in other places, He came back to his own country, around some of his folks, the same people he grew up with, worked in the vineyards with, and went to festivals with.

Those people missed the shift because they were trying to underestimate who Jesus was.

They missed the shift because they were asking, "Is He the carpenter's son? Doesn't His brothers and sisters live here?

> *And it came to pass, that when Jesus had finished these parables, he departed thence.*
>
> *And when he was come into his own country, he taught them in their synagogue, insomuch that they were astonished, and said, Whence hath this man this wisdom, and these mighty works?*
>
> *Is not this the carpenter's son? is not his mother called Mary? and his brethren, James, and Joses, and Simon, and Judas?*
>
> *And his sisters, are they not all with us? Whence then hath this man all these things?*
>
> *And they were offended in him. But Jesus said unto them, a prophet is not without honour, save in his own country, and in his own house.*
>
> *Matthew 13: 53-57 KJV*

You may have left your house one way, but when you step out in your visions, you will return differently.

When you begin to say, "I see the glass as half full, instead of half empty," others will say, "You don't know what you are talking about. That glass is half empty."

When you begin to say, "I'm coming out of this," others will say, "I don't know how. I don't know why you think you will succeed."

The shift will leave some people behind. You will have to surround yourself with new people. You will hang with the people that will pull the best out of you and not the worst. In this shift, you won't be the same. People may not understand, but you must keep pressing toward the mark of a higher calling. Your destiny is tied up in this shift. Your marriage is tied up in this shift, your finances, your ministry, and your children.

It's time for the young people to catch this shift. The enemy knows that if the young people catch the shift, it's going to be in serious trouble. Freedom from generational curses is in the shift. I'm talking about a shift that will cause a life-changing experience, a change that will release the unlimited blessings of God to you. I'm talking about a shift that will bring favor to rest upon your life.

You are special, and God wants to keep advancing you through your ideas, visions, businesses, families, jobs, ministry, health, and wealth. You must remember that you have done great things, but you have more greatness that has not been released. Don't stop at the success you have enjoyed. Others are depending on you now. Protect your gifts.

"Bring ye all the tithes into the storehouse, that there may be meat in mine house, and prove me now herewith, saith the LORD of hosts, if I will not open you the windows of heaven, and pour you out a blessing, that there shall not be room enough to receive it."
Malachi 3:10 KJV

PRINCIPLE XI:
WINNING FINANCES

Finances are in everything you do. You will make some transactions daily involving finances. You can rest assured that you will deal with something every day regarding your finances, whether big or small. No one wants to be in bondage with finances, so even if you have plenty of money or not as much as others, you will need to know how to manage it.

It is God's will that you be prosperous. He came that we could have life and have it abundantly. We are supposed to be able to enjoy the good of the earth, go on vacations, and be able to live and not have to struggle. Some people may not be as fortunate but they're wise in handling it and can do the things they love to do. On the other hand, some people make more, but don't know how to budget their resources to be able to enjoy life. Understanding your finances and areas of growth is very important if you wish to see yourself winning in this area.

Learn to Handle Finances

Many people are not good with finances. They haven't been taught or given consistent guidance on properly handling finances. Most people learn as they go and began to get better at handling their finances. I believe that the earlier good financial management is instilled in youth, the better. My parents sat me down and taught me how to write a check. They taught me how to estimate how much I would spend and how much to save. In the beginning, just like most people, I would spend it all.

My mom says that you will always find something to spend your money on, but you must learn how to save for yourself. After you take your tithes out, take another portion out and do not touch it. Over time, I caught on to saving techniques and saw the value of saving.

To help advance your future, you should start studying finances. Learn about spending wisely, saving, investing, return on your money, IRA's, etc. I always like to look at the return on investment. I learned that anybody could spend money, but not everybody had the knowledge and information to save or get a return on money. Having winning finances requires that you understand how you treat your money will be a determining factor in your growth. You must address your area of weakness in finances, whether you like shopping, going out to restaurants, or other kinds of spending. Once you address your weakness, then you can begin to manage one thing at a time. You may start by eating out less or choosing inexpensive restaurants to start the process. Every good thing must start somewhere, and you can make it begin with little adjustments over time. Once you get to a level of where you can eat out daily do it, if you choose. Learn the value of preserving and not wasting money.

Saving

Learning to save two or three dollars out of every ten dollars was one of the lessons my parents shared with us. They wanted to start us early, teaching how to save so we could break the curse of living from paycheck to paycheck and borrowing to make ends meet. My parents said that finances are a struggle for people, even good people. They wanted us to appreciate the finances we had, but also to have wisdom of spending it.

I had to learn as a child that even though my parents gave me a roof over my head, food to eat, and clothes to wear, if I wanted to go to the movies or skating, I had to save money for those things. I begin to encourage myself to save money. Get yourself in a place as a young person where you can start saving, so when you graduate from high school, you may not have to get student loans for college. You could be in a position to pay for college yourself. I learned that youth respond better if we challenge them even at a young age to learn how to manage every dollar that they get.

Connection and Budgeting

When I grew up, my dad understood that our family could use growth in our finances, he connected with someone who dealt with finances daily, and he surrounded himself with like-minded people who wanted to do better financially. The people in your circle can help you become better at what you do or keep you down. Growth is always important no matter how old you are, how much you know, or how much you have acquired. Finance is a desired area we all want to see improved.

According to the Bible, we should be the lender and not the borrower.

("The Lord shall open unto thee his good treasure, the heaven to give the rain unto thy land in his season, and to bless all the work of thine hand: and thou shalt lend unto many nations, and thou shalt not borrow." Deuteronomy 28:12 KJV.)

To acquire such a position, we must tap into that way of thinking.

Repeat this affirmation to yourself:
"I'm a lender and not a borrower."

You must begin somewhere. If you save $10 at a time, you will gain momentum or establish a habit of saving. Then you can move up to saving $20 and from there to $50.

Give yourself a budget and try to stand by it. Watch what you spend daily and see where you can improve. You will soon be in a position to enjoy your money, pay your bills and do all the extra things that you want to do.

Preparation brings elevation.

"Turn again, and tell Hezekiah the captain of my people, Thus saith the Lord, the God of David thy father, I have heard thy prayer, I have seen thy tears: behold, I will heal thee: on the third day thou shalt go up unto the house of the Lord."
2 Kings 20:5 KJV

PRINCIPLE XII:
WINNING HEALTH

Health is the key to a happy life. Managing your health is very important. Truthfully, we can all do something to improve our eating style, getting the proper rest, and taking care of any current health conditions. In our family, we travel extensively; therefore, we may not always get the opportunity to eat right, exercise, and rest. Over time, this lifestyle began to affect my father. He was always up late working. He would continue such hard work throughout the night to get the job completed. Since we are an independent label, and I am an independent artist, my dad takes care of all the business and day-to-day transactions. As an independent, he knew that our company had to operate at the same level as the major labels. Being a small business meant he had to do masses of work in-house. My dad studied every aspect of the industry, which required time and dedication.

There were times when we were up late in the night and we would turn to eating a great deal of junk food, because that was the most avaiable items we could get our hands on at the time. My dad's body then came under attack; improper eating and lack of rest took a complete toll his body. One day as we were traveling, he became sick, and he chose not to see a doctor at that time. When we returned home, he finally resulted to visiting his doctor. When he was examined, the doctors stated his condition was all because of the lack of rest and improper diet. The condition of not having enough rest then caused him to be borderline diabetic. He was placed on bed rest for a week with the pleasure of eating healthy and nutritious food.

We learned that in the midst of working the assignment and being blessed, that you must incorporate the proper precaution for your body's well-being to enjoy your years. We could have everything in the world and not be able to enjoy it. We understood that we needed a true balance in every aspect of our lives.

This scripture became one of our favorite:

"Beloved, I wish above all things that thou mayest prosper and be in health, even as thy soul prospereth."

3 John 2 KJV

God wanted us to prosper in all areas of our life, including our health. As our soul prospers, it is meant for our natural life to thrive. Living unhealthy, with financial issues, depression, low self-esteem, and unhappiness is not what God wants for us.

You are supposed to live absolute in every area of your life. His word says, He wants us to prosper in all areas of our life. Do not let traditions mislead you the way you have seen others do it or even by your way of thinking. God desires to see all of his people blessed and living a joyous life. Whether your health issue is short term or long term, you must take a positive approach to win the fight.

Many great people have experienced health issues beyond their control.

I will never forget when Sheilah Belle, a good friend in the industry, called my dad to invite me to be a guest at a special event that she was having entitled, "The Gift." She wanted me to sing my songs,"You're Bigger" and "Greater Is Coming." She didn't give any specifics about the event, other than, "I need you to come and be apart." My dad communicated to her we would attend.

Sheilah Belle has worked in the field of broadcast entertainment and news for over 25 years. She is a radio host, producer, entrepreneur, concert promoter, media consultant and a much sought-after speaker.

In addition to being a mid-day host for Radio One's Praise 104.7 FM in Richmond, Va., one of the most powerful gospel stations in the country, she is also the C.E.O. of The Belle Report, LaBelle & Associates. She produces and anchors The Belle Report Radio show that airs in nearly 60 markets. She is one of the most respected multi-media journalists within the industry and has become a highly requested inspirational speaker. She continues to grow her ministry to inspire and uplift others. As a result, she is now doing more speaking engagements in churches, music workshops, conferences, and non-profit organizations with topics ranging from ministry to social media.

With all her accolades and her extensive work, she, like many, has run into an issue with her health. The way she approached her issue is what characterized her as a winner.

When I attended her event, I was not yet aware of her health issues. At first glance, I did not recognize her. She was taking treatments for cancer, but with such perserverance and selflessness, she stood before us hosting an event that was blessing others dealing with the same issue. What I liked the most about seeing her at this event was her "winning attitude"— she was healed and winning. She smiled through almost the entire production. She took on the attitude to win against cancer. That night, I watched her inspire many as they came one after another, sharing their stories of overcoming the fight against cancer. She could have just said, "I have my own problems." Yet she did not let that hinder her from opening her heart, arms and spirit to bless others. She never showed pity upon herself. Sheilah Belle took on a winning heart to share and help others, even when it seemed as if she would need the care herself. With her winning faith and winning attitude, she is now cancer free.

God bless you, Sheilah Belle!

With prayer, faith, works, belief, and a right attitude, you can overcome sickness. I recall the story of Hezekiah, who was terminally ill, in the book of 2 Kings, Chapter 20. Hezekiah prayed and had the right attitude; therefore, God interrupted the plans of death he had over his life.

God is about to interrupt the natural flow on your behalf.

The prophet Isaiah visited Hezekiah in the first verse and said to him, this is what the Lord says, "Give your household instructions, for you are about to die, you will not get well." *("Thus saith the Lord, Set thine house in order; for thou shalt die, and not live.")* Now, you must remember God sent the prophet Isaiah to Hezekiah. In this case, the word was from God. I want you to understand how serious the word spoken to Hezekiah was. Death was upon him. He was a few breaths away from his end, several heartbeats away from his last, one or two steps from his last walk. So yes, it was natural to say, prepare for the funeral at this point. Hezekiah needed a supernatural miracle. Down in the second and third verse of 2 Kings, Chapter 20, Hezekiah turned to the wall and prayed to the Lord. Hezekiah didn't know anything else to do at that moment but pray. He didn't try to get the best doctor or the best medicine. He didn't gather his family around to hear his final say. Hezekiah didn't begin to divide his goods amongst his people, but he prayed.

Prayer works when money doesn't. Prayer helps when family is not available. Prayer works when your education is can't. When a spaceship guided by an astronaut can't reach the highest altitude, prayer can because it is the direct line to heaven. Prayer can reach the heavens when the tallest ladder in the world cannot. Prayer can reach the heavens when the tallest building in the world cannot. Hezekiah began to remind God of how he served Him and carried out His will.

Now, this is where *grace* and *mercy* kicks in. God heard his prayer. God told Isaiah to go to Hezekiah and tell him, "I have heard your prayer. I've seen your tears, "look, I will heal you." God's grace showed up to demonstrate how beautiful He is. His mercy demonstrated that He hears the cry of His children.

Thank God for *grace* and *mercy*. God interrupted the natural flow. You must know that mercy will bless you even when you don't deserve it. When you read a little further, after Isaiah told Hezekiah that he was restored, Hezekiah asked, "What shall be the sign?" Isaiah asked him if he wanted God to move the shadow forward ten degrees or back ten degrees. Let me paraphrase, Hezekiah said, it's nothing for the shadow to move forward ten degrees. You've got to understand that the only way the shadow can move positions is by the sun changing its position. It's nothing for the sun to go forward ten degrees. I want you to make it go backward, Isaiah cried out to God, and God brought the shadow back ten degrees

God interrupt the natural flow, and He also reversed the time for Hezekiah. So, in other words, Hezekiah got a two-in-one miracle. He received two miracles at one time.

In Daniel 6:16-28, when Daniel was in the den with the hungry lion, he was supposed to die, but God interrupted the natural flow of hunger and shut the lion's mouth. The people who tried to have him killed were put to death instead, God reversed it.

The three Hebrew boys were thrown into the fiery furnace, and it was turned up seven times hotter than usual (Daniel 3:19). They were supposed to be burned to ashes, but God interrupted the natural flow of heat, they were released from the furnace without smelling like smoke and without a burn. People wanted them to be decimated, but God reversed it.

In Deuteronomy 8:4, the children of Israel walked in the wilderness for many years. God interrupted the natural flow of fabrics and linens and did not allow their clothes or shoes to wear down. God is interrupting a matter on your behalf. Everything that was supposed to exterminate you, God is about to reverse for it.

Some things you're going through have no regards to you, but God is using the situation for the purpose of helping others. People around you may be spectators and doubted who you are. So, God almighty chose to put you in the furnace and the lion's den for you to see His favor in your life. Be thankful for your experiences, because it's going to walk you into your *greater* place.

Doctors may have told you that your death is at hand. You may have lost your job, and may be one month away from losing your home. Your car may be in the process of being repossessed, and some of you may be losing a court battle and to know you're one court appearance from the final verdict. You may have a family member on drugs, and it's been declared that there's no possible way for recovery. Your home has been shattered, and it is now considered unsalvageable.

You are now one day from losing your mind and have concluded the only fix will be a supernatural miracle.

God says this isn't the time for you to give up, but this is the time for you to pray. Why should you pray? Prayer reaches God, and when prayer reaches God, He hears His children, and He began interrupting situations. God is interrupting the plans of the enemy now.

Hezekiah could have turned around and given up, but he obtained an attitude of "God I'm your child." What Hezekiah said touched the heart of God. You may have a health issue, but your attitude determines the toll that it will take on you. You will "win" the fight for your health. You are victorious. Health issues or any other issues that come your way will not defeat you. Take on the attitude that "I can make it. I am going to make it."

"Give, and it shall be given unto you; good measure, pressed down, and shaken together, and running over, shall men give into your bosom. For with the same measure that ye mete withal it shall be measured to you again."
Luke 6:38 KJV

PRINCIPLE XIII:
TITHER, GIVER, SOWER

Tithing and being a giver, and a sower has been a significant responsibility for me and my family. In our everyday walk we had to step out in faith, believing and trusting the vision, tithing, giving, and sowing which is an essential factor in our lives. Planting seeds and being able to watch them manifest later is always amazing. Your prayer life, tithing, giving, sowing, and works help produce your harvest. For Principle XI: Finances, we used the scripture Malachi 3:10: "Bring ye all the tithes into the storehouse..."

If you tithe, you have just challenged God to open the windows of heaven for you.

At the beginning of the year, people begin to prepare taxes. After they submit their taxes, many people expect a refund. Tax refunds come only once a year. I believe, without a doubt when you tithe, God will make your entire year feel better than a tax return. By tithing, you also block the devourer from taking your profit.

- Tither—Takes care of (Kingdom business) supplies the necessities of the ministry.
- Giver—Gives from the heart.
- Sower—Plants seeds, and every seed yield a harvest of its kind!

I believe my family life wouldn't be what it is today, if we weren't tithing, giving, and sowing seeds. I have seen miraculous things happen because we stepped out on faith to give, sow, and pay our tithes. We learned early to tithe on the little money we had. Even when our income increased, we continued to tithe.

We always have a discerning spirit when it came to sowing; we would wait for the right moment. If you trust God with His portion, He will trust you and increase your portion. God will tend to your every need... Remember Luke 6:38.

I found that some people may not believe in what we call tithing, giving, and sowing, but they still practice it. *"God is no respecter of persons" (Acts 10:34)*, but if they are operating by the principles, He will honor it.

As far back as I can remember, at three, four, and five years old, our parents taught us about tithing. Tithing was one of the first things that I learned when it came to money. Learning how to tithe early in life taught me how to budget. My parents would give my siblings and me $10 or $20, and they would ask, "Did you take out God's portion?" They wanted us to understand early about having the responsibility of giving. No matter what I had, I knew I could not touch His portion.

We quickly took on the teaching of being responsible with tithing, whenever my siblings and I received money, we would give our tithes before our parents would even ask for them. The principle of tithing was embedded in us. Next, we learned that after we give our portion to God, we must put a portion away for ourselves.

I have seen our family expand beyond our comprehension because of our tithing. We see consistent growth because of our tithing. My dad says he wants us to understand the importance of giving God's portion first so that we could have a sense of peace.

7 Steps to Victory

1. Tithe, sow, and give
2. Define your win
3. Use your time to produce your visions
4. Keep balance in your life
5. Respect others
6. Use words that commands your atmosphere to win
7. Protect your gifts

"Come now therefore, I pray thee, curse me this people; for they are too mighty for me: peradventure I shall prevail, that we may smite them, and that I may drive them out of the land: for I wot that he whom thou blessest is blessed, and he whom thou cursest is cursed."
Numbers 22:6 KJV

PRINCIPLE XIV: WINNING RISE

Satan the adversary, the accuser, the competitor, the robber, and the deceiver, tries to compete against God. He is an opponent. He goes against everything God does and says. He goes against the truth. Let truth be known, Satan hates the truth. He is a spirit, and wants to be like God. He needs a vehicle, a body, to operate through to carry out his plan. The devil knows you as well as you know yourself. That's why he keeps presenting things to you that opposes the truth of who you are so that you won't see or recognize your true identity.

The devil knows that you are a child of the covenant. He knows that you are a child of the promise, but he wants you to see the opposite of your promise and be filled with doubt, worry, and depression.

He knows you are victorious, so the enemy tries to show you the opposite which is failure and defeat. He wants you to see yourself as a loser, or a nobody. He knows that you are healed, but he shows sickness, pain, addiction and hurt.

If he had the power, he would keep you blinded and weak to his lies.

The story of Balak and Balaam from the book of Numbers gives an anecdote about fear.

"And Balak the son of Zippor saw all that Israel had done to the Amorites. And Moab was sore afraid of the people, because they were many: and Moab was distressed because of the children of Israel.

> *And Moab said unto the elders of Midian, now shall this company lick up all that are round about us, as the ox licketh up the grass of the field. And Balak the son of Zippor was king of the Moabites at that time.*
>
> *He sent messengers therefore unto Balaam the son of Beor to Pethor, which is by the river of the land of the children of his people, to call him, saying, Behold, there is a people come out from Egypt: behold, they cover the face of the earth, and they abide over against me:*
>
> *Come now therefore, I pray thee, curse me this people; for they are too mighty for me: peradventure I shall prevail, that we may smite them, and that I may drive them out of the land: for I wot that he whom thou blessest is blessed, and he whom thou cursest is cursed."*
>
> *Numbers 22: 2-6*

Balak knew he couldn't stop Israel, so he sent for a man called Balaam to come and curse Israel. It was known in the land. If Balaam cursed you; you would be cursed. If he blessed you, you were blessed. Balak sent for this man, Balaam, to encourage him to curse the Israelites. Don't be surprised how far the enemy will go to try to stop you from moving into your *greater* place.

Balak was intimidated by Israel's growth. He watching them defeat the enemies they encountered and it intimidated him.

"Intimidated" means to make timid or fearful: frighten (Webster dictionary)

Balak became fearful because of what he saw. When the enemy sees that you are progressing or moving, he is intimidated. When he sees that you are walking in high places, the head and not the tail, the lender and not the borrower, or the heir to your inheritance he is intimidated.

He becomes intimidated and calls forth the spirit of Balaam to work against you and to speak against what God has created. Balak wanted Balaam to curse the people by speaking death into the atmosphere. Balak felt as if the word of death was released into the atmosphere, it would kill the work the children of Israel had accomplished.

The enemy always tries to use someone to speak against you and the word of God that's over your life, to cause you to waver and doubt who you are and what you were called to do. No matter what he does, you have to know that if God has blessed you, no opposition can deny you your blessings.

Declaration

I declare right now that the devil is a liar, and the true identity of the people of God is being revealed in this hour. No longer will the people of God be imprisoned by the evil ways of the enemy.

If you are an individual that the enemy has attacked and tried to rob and make you believe that you are not the person God created, you to be. I want you to take a look at yourself now and say, "My identity is about to change."

If the enemy has been making you feel that you are a nobody, know that's the opposite of who you are.

If the enemy has been making you feel worthless, it's because he knows how valuable you are.

If he has been showing you poverty, it's because he really sees wealth upon you.

If the enemy has been showing you failure, it's because he sees the greatness upon your life.

The ultimate plans that Satan has is to send signs and messengers that will clog your vision and your ability to see the greatness that God placed inside of you. You are an overcomer.

Some of you are just like Israel. You may have a mighty move going on in your life, and you are taking the enemy by a storm, but just as you are reaching your destination, the enemy tries to throw darts to stop you.

I want to reiterate that you must be careful of what you release into the atmosphere. You could be cursing yourself or blessing yourself. If a person is always saying, "I'm broke," he or she has spoken against prosperity.

That's why the Bible says, *"Death and life are in the power of your tongue: and they that love it shall eat the fruit thereof."*

Proverbs 18:21 KJV

You will eat the fruit of which what you declare. So, if you speak death over your money, you shall eat the fruit of having no money

That's why you must speak: "Even though I don't have it now, I am still rich. My wealth is still coming to me." So, you can eat the fruit of the rich.

Joel 3:10 (KJV) says, *"...Let the weak say; I am strong."*

Even though you are weak, you are still strong. You must say, "I'm strong," even in your most vulnerable moment. You must speak against everything that the enemy is speaking over your life.

People may hassle or choose not to befriend you— just because, situations in your life may be going all wrong—but what's actually happening is that you have become a threat to the enemy. The enemy wants and is trying to curse you. On the contrary, the enemy can't curse what God has blessed.

You may find yourself on the front line, under attack and you finally realize it's the enemy. The enemy seems to never show his face until you institute pursuing everything that entails your purpose. The enemy watches from a distance, keeping you under surveillance, as you rise out of your old ways returning to your purpose. He then urgently rushes to chase after your anointing and character.

That's why it's important to hide in the presence of God. The enemy will chase you on your job, home, or school, etc., but it's so awesome to know he can't chase you in the presence of God.

In Numbers 22:20, God came to Balaam and told him to go with them.

> *"And Balaam rose up in the morning, and saddled his ass, and went with the princes of Moab."*
> *And God's anger was kindled because he went: and the angel of the LORD stood in the way for an adversary against him....*
> *Numbers 22:21-22*

In the 35th verse, God gave Balaam permission to go, but God also told him to speak His word.

Sometime during the night, Balaam had begun to think about the money and wealth he would collect if he went and cursed Jacob and Israel. The wealth was more important than what God spoke. He decided to speak a curse over Israel, with the thoughts prospering.

But God!!!

As Balaam was riding along the road; his donkey saw the angel of the Lord, and the donkey began to reject Balaam's instruction to the point where Balaam wanted to destroy the donkey. Finally, the Lord opened Balaam's eyes. The angel of the Lord spoke to Balaam and told him if the donkey had not turned aside, I would have killed you.

Can't you see that every time the enemy was on his way to try to destroy you, God put an angel in the way? Every time the enemy hopped in his car to come to attack your name, God let an angel cause his car to fail.

When the enemy said, "I got my car fixed now and I'm on my way to execute you," God sent an angel and caused him to have a blowout. WOW! How he loves you.

God blocks everything that's oblivious to you, which was sent to eradicate everything and everyone that's associated with you. God told Balaam to tell the people, "How can I curse whom God has not cursed? And how can I denounce whom he has not denounced."

You see Balak came to Balaam four or five times, taking him to several different places, trying to urge him to curse Israel. No matter which side he chose, from the high to the low, from the east to the west, they were still pronounced not cursed. The enemy will try to come from all angles to attack you.

No matter what the enemy has introduced, he is only going to see what God called you to be. When he comes from the West, he sees "not cursed." When he comes from the East, he sees "prosperity upon you." When he comes from the South, he sees "God's chosen vessel." When he comes from North, he sees the greatness upon you.

He sees the next King on the rise.

He sees the next Inventor on the rise.

He sees the next Designer on the rise.

He sees the next History Maker on the rise.

He sees the next Visionaries on the rise.

All the attacks that the enemy was trying use on Israel began when he saw Jacob and Israel on the rise.

So now the enemy sees you on the rise. That's why your money, family, and mind is now so very important to him. You now know that you are under attack because the enemy has seen your greatness.

Look at Jeremiah 28.

God sent a word to Prophet Jeremiah and told him to tell Hananiah that he caused the people to trust a lie.

> *Then said the prophet Jeremiah unto Hananiah the prophet, hear now, Hananiah; The Lord hath not sent thee; but thou makest this people to trust in a lie.*
>
> *Therefore, thus saith the Lord; Behold, I will cast thee from off the face of the earth: this year thou shalt die, because thou hast taught rebellion against the Lord.*
>
> *So Hananiah the prophet died the same year in the seventh month.*
> *Jeremiah 28: 15-17*

The word the enemy has released over your life is a lie.

He said you couldn't be free.

He said that you were not called.

He said that you were a nobody.

He said you were never going to write that book.

You weren't going to write the Number One song.

You weren't going to be successful.

He said you were going to have riches.

He also said your ministry wasn't going to grow.

God told Jeremiah to tell Hananiah that he was going to die. This year every lie that came up against you will die. That curse shall die. The lack that you are experiencing shall die.

What's significant about the death of Hananiah is that the month when he died was in the seventh month. Seven signifies the day God rested.

God is getting ready to rest upon you like never before, and everything that God told you, you have to believe that it's going to happen.

BONUS:
21 DAYS OF WINNING VERSES

I have assembled these verses for you to speak over your life.

Day 1: "I am more than a conqueror."
"Nay, in all these things we are more than conquerors through him that loved us."
Romans 8:37

Day 2: "It's working in my favor."
"And we know that all things work together for good to them that love God, to them who are the called according to his purpose."
Romans 8:28

Day 3: "I can win."
"I can do all things through Christ which strengtheneth me."
Philippians 4:13

Day 4: "I'm healed by the stripes of Jesus."
"But he was wounded for our transgressions, he was bruised for our iniquities: the chastisement of our peace was upon him, and with his stripes, we are healed."
Isaiah 53:5

Day 5: "I pray."
"And in the morning, rising up a great while before day, he went out, and departed into a solitary place, and there prayed."
Mark 1:35

Day 6: "The battle is already won."
And all this assembly shall know that the Lord saveth not with sword and spear: for the battle is the Lord's, and he will give you into our hands.
1 Samuel 17:47

Day 7: "I acknowledge my struggle is not against flesh and blood."
"For we wrestle not against flesh and blood, but against principalities, against powers, against the rulers of the darkness of this world, against spiritual wickedness in high places."
Ephesians 6:12

Day 8: "My enemy has been disarmed and embarrassed."
"And having spoiled principalities and powers, he made a shew of them openly, triumphing over them in it."
Colossians 2:15

Day 9: "I am triumphant."
"Now thanks be unto God, which always causeth us to triumph in Christ, and maketh manifest the savour of his knowledge by us in every place."
2 Corinthians 2:14

Day 10: "I am chosen and dearly loved by Christ."
"According as he hath chosen us in him before the foundation of the world, that we should be holy and without blame before him in love:"
Ephesians 1:4

Day 11: "I am the righteousness of God in Christ."
"For he hath made him to be sin for us, who knew no sin; that we might be made the righteousness of God in him."
2 Corinthians 5:21

Day 12: "My fears are defeated."
"For God hath not given us the spirit of fear; but of power, and of love, and of a sound mind."
2 Timothy 1:7

Day 13: "I overcome the world."
"For whatsoever is born of God overcometh the world: and this is the victory that overcometh the world, even our faith."
1 John 5:4

Day 14: "I am chosen and dearly loved by Christ."
"According as he hath chosen us in him before the foundation of the world, that we should be holy and without blame before him in love:"
Ephesians 1:4

Day 15: "I am a citizen of Heaven and seated in heavenly places right now."
"And hath raised us up together, and made us sit together in heavenly places in Christ Jesus:"
Ephesians 2:6

Day 16: "The Lord, my God, fights for me."
"For the Lord, your God is he that goeth with you, to fight for you against your enemies, to save you."
Deuteronomy 20:4

Day 17: "I won't faint."
"And let us not be weary in well doing: for in due season we shall reap, if we faint not."
Galatians 6:9

Day 18: "My God is for me."
"What shall we then say to these things? If God be for us, who can be against us?"
Romans 8:31

Day 19: I give God all of the glory."
"Let my mouth be filled with thy praise and with thy honour all the day."
Psalms 71:8

Day 20: "I will get through this."
"We are troubled on every side, yet not distressed; we are perplexed, but not in despair; Persecuted, but not forsaken; cast down, but not destroyed;"
2 Corinthians 4:8-9

Day 21: "It's only a shadow."
"Yea, though I walk through the valley of the shadow of death,
I will fear no evil: for thou art with me;
thy rod and thy staff they comfort me."
Psalms 23:4

All the scriptures for the 21 days are from the King James Version of the Bible.

SPECIAL MESSAGES

Stretch to Win

You need to stretch yourself in many cases to receive and walk in greatness. What I mean to stretch is to come out of the comfortable place where you have been. Stretching your faith will help you to break through. Many people have suffered because of the economy in the last few years, but God is going to use the individuals that have been trusting in Him as examples.

Even though the stock market may crash, the word that God has spoken over your life will never crash. I know the Dow goes up and down, but His word does not change. I know when you lose your money in an investment; you can't get a return. Although, if you sacrifice, and make a portion for God, you shall gain everything back and some. I want you to know that every promise and every word that God has spoken over your life, it shall be.

It has been prophesied that some of you will be leaders have an excellent job, beautiful homes, nice cars, your family would be saved, and that you would be a millionaire, but you are still waiting.

God is redirecting your faith toward Him, so that He can do it. There are two things that are important in your stretch. One is waiting on God, and two is seeking God.

"…*They that wait upon the Lord shall renew their strength."* (Isaiah 40:31 KJV) Waiting is the process by which God is working for you. You are not working, but instead you are seeking him. Sometimes in the waiting place, it seems that you are praying, fasting and going to church, but nothing is happening. Just because you don't see it now, does not mean it's not going to happen. It takes patience when you are waiting on God. It's the place of preparation.

It's also the place where the enemy uses his distractions against you, including doubt and anxiety. He uses people to keep you from focusing. It's the place where the enemy wants you to leave, because the longer you hang out in the place of preparation, the more you will trust God.

So, he begins to attack you in the waiting place by telling you nothing is happening.

He tries to tell you that you need to take it out of the hands of God instead of waiting on God.

He wants you to feel uncomfortable in the waiting place. So, he now tries to get you away from your safety zone in the waiting place, where God's presence is greatly upon you. The waiting place is where the millionaires are made, leaders are made, houses are built, college is paid off, new careers are happening, and even better than that, destiny is becoming a reality.

You are learning in this place how to handle the blessing, so that you can receive your blessing. You want the blessings; you want to know how to handle the blessings, so you won't lose the blessing.

Seeking Him While Waiting

The Bible says, *but seek ye first the kingdom of God, and his righteousness; and all these things shall be added unto you.*

Matthew 6:33 KJV

Sometimes unintentionally or intentionally, we swap the order. We get caught up with the things around us, and we begin to seek the things first, instead of seeking God.

That's how the enemy will try to come in and try to kill your purpose.

He's saying, "If I can keep them focused on the things and not God, then I can get them away from their waiting place. You must redirect your focus to seeking him first. You must trust God even in the waiting place.

Because of your faith stretch, things in your life shift.

Because of your faith stretch, circumstances are about to change.

Because of your faith stretch, somebody in your home is about receive a miracle.

Because of your faith stretch, healing is taking place in your family.

This stretch of faith is causing a supernatural move.

The doctor is going to say, "I don't know how it happened."

The banker is going to say, "I don't know how you got approved."

Your school is going to say, "Your student loan is paid in full."

The court is going to say, "Release this child."

This stretch is going to cause an increase.

That's why the enemy doesn't want your faith to be built up.

Because he knows all the things that are coming to you.

He doesn't want to see you go from "empty" to "full."

He doesn't want to see you leave from this place to your greater place.

It's important that you Stretch this season in your life.

Greater Is Coming

Greater comes from the root word "great."

Great means large in number, unusual in degree, intensity and power.

Often, when *greatness* is upon you, you will have to experience greater difficulties. With *greatness* upon your life, the intensity and degree of things you will have to deal with are much higher. You become use to dealing with one or two things, now you have five to seven things that are going crazy in your life

But one underlining fact comes from this, and that is: "***Greater Is Coming*.**"

Some people are now in uncomfortable places in their lives.

However, I want you to understand that this place you are in now, is to show you what God is capable of doing for you. For a long time, people have trusted in their jobs or other sources. They didn't totally recognize God to be the source of all their being.

You were promoted. It wasn't that you were so wonderful, but it was God.

You got a new home. It wasn't because of all the money you were bringing in, but it was God.

This season we are in, is pushing us to a place that we must trust God.

I heard a young lady testify once about how the enemy broke into her home and stole from her, then came back again and stole her car. One day while working she lost the diamond out of her ring. In the midst of all of that, she still told God, "Thank you!" Why? Because she knew the God that she serves.

You may have lost somethings in your life, but still tell God, "Thank you!" --- because now He has *greater* coming to you.

So be thankful for your loss, because now you can begin to regain. God is preparing you for *greater, and* that's why you must tell Him, "Thank you!" Thank him in advance.

The Bible says,

"Preach the word; be instant in season, out of season...."

2 Timothy 4:2 KJV

So, if you can tell God, "Thank you!" when it seems out of season; where you lost your job, where you got evicted, where you have no money, "Thank you" just told God, you can trust me with a home or no home, with diamonds or no diamonds, with a job or no job, with family or without family.

God wants us to have these things, but you have to trust Him even in a losing situation, to know that *greater* is coming.

Job trusted God in a losing situation. Job lost his oxen, his sheep, his camels, his seven sons and three daughters. Sickness struck his body. Yet, Job still trusted God.

You must understand, that if it had not been for your loss, you wouldn't have known that you can handle these thing that you're dealing with.

You chose to tell God, "Thank you!" in this place, instead of feeling sorry for yourself.

"Thank you" just told God, "I don't know where you're taking me this time, but God I still trust you. I don't know what you're doing for me in this season, but God I still trust you."

The Bible says,

"Many are the afflictions of the righteous: but the Lord delivereth him out of them all."
Psalms 34: 19 KJV

The righteous will be afflicted, but God will not leave you that way. His word declares that the Lord will deliver you out of them all.

Every righteous person who has been afflicted needs to say, "Get ready, because God is delivering me." You must see your way out, before it happens, just as the prophet did in Isaiah 40.

When Israel was going through a hard time, the prophet stopped looking at the situation he was in, and he began to declare that Israel had been pardoned, and began to say, *"Prepare ye the way of the Lord!"*

"The voice of him that crieth in the wilderness, prepare ye the way of the LORD, make straight in the desert a highway for our God."
Isaiah 40:3 KJV

If you have been in a tough place in your life, go and prepare the way for the Lord.

The reason God hasn't shown up is that you haven't prepared the way for Him to come.

How do you prepare the way for God?

1. You have to trust Him.
2. You have to pray.
3. You have to step back and let God do it.
4. You have to believe that He's allowing this for your greater.

Not all things happen because you have done something wrong. Some things happen so you can learn how to trust God and He can bring the best out of you.

It's like, what the olive goes through to make olive oil. An olive has to go through three stages

1. The shaking —- Some of you might have gone through your shaking already, and some of you might be going through it now.
2. The beating —- Some of you feel that you have been beaten up.
3. The pressing—- Some of you feel that you already have been pressed down.

After the olive has gone through its final stages, after being shaken up/beaten up, pressed down, the olive releases all the oil. So, all the pressure that you are feeling, it's just God pressing *greater* out of you. God merely took you through all three stages to make the finest oil.

The inspiration for writing Greater Is Coming was from the when a lot of people were experiencing such a hard time with the economy, such as homes foreclosing and job losses. Watching people how they were dealing with all the things happening in life brought about the song Greater Is Coming.

If it had not been for your shaking, if it had not been for your beating, if it had not been for your pressing, your oil wouldn't have been able to flow. You wouldn't have known that you could handle what you're going through now.

In the Bible days, oil was one of the first sources of money used to pay for things.

Now, God has taken you back to the beginning — that the oil that's been pressed out of you will pay for all the things the enemy said you couldn't have.

This oil that's being pressed out of you will bring prosperity.

This oil will cause your family to be healed.

This oil that's upon you will birth your ministry in another place.

This oil that's on you now will cause you to write a Number One selling book.

This oil that's on you now will cause you to write that Number One Billboard song.

In the Bible, not only was oil used as money, but it was used and still being used to anoint.

This oil that's has been pressed out of you has anointed you for greatness.

This oil has anointed you for the position.

This oil has anointed you to write.

This oil has anointed you to lead.

This oil flowing out of you will cause people to say, "How did you do that?"

A many times people don't see that what they are experiencing is for their *greater*. They see the pain, the hurt. They hear the lies. Truthfully, the lie that was told on you, was to make you stop, so you wouldn't experience your *greater place*.

The enemy is after your greatness

You have to thank God for the shaking.

You have to thank God for the beating.

You have to thank Him for the pressing.

Because now your oil is ready to flow.

He's preparing you for greater.

He shook you for greater to flow.

You felt a beating .

He had to press you, for your greater anointing, greater power, greater destiny.

The doctor may have given up on you.

You may have lost your job.

That person walks out of your life.

Now your healing is going to be even more greater. Your business is going to be even greater. Your ideas will be greater. Your finances will be greater.

You're getting ready to have greater on top of greater.

Even though you had to experience the tears, loss, and hurt, I want to speak into your life that something Greater Is Coming.

"Then said Elijah unto the people, I, even I only, remain a prophet of the Lord; but Baal's prophets are four hundred and fifty men."

1 Kings 18:22 KJV

> *"And he put the wood in order, and cut the bullock in pieces, and laid him on the wood, and said, fill four barrels with water, and pour it on the burnt sacrifice, and on the wood.*
>
> *And he said, Do it the second time. And they did it the second time. And he said, Do it the third time. And they did it the third time.*
>
> *And the water ran round about the altar; and he filled the trench also with water.*
>
> *1 Kings 18:33-35 KJV*

Elijah stretched his faith for fire on a bullock and wood that he had 12 barrels of water poured on. He also filled the trench with water, after he repaired the altar that the prophets of Baal destroyed. Elijah, not only had to speak against one prophet, but there were 450 prophets of Baal who were going against his word.

When one person speaks against you, some of you begin to doubt. By the time a second person speaks against you, you are ready to quit believing God for your purpose, (your *greater*).

Imagine declaring a word and 450 people coming against the word. The difference between you and Elijah is that, he was not about to argue the word. Elijah put it all on God to do it.

Tell yourself, "the word that's over your life, it is on God to perform it." All you have to do is stretch your faith, work, and watch God do it.

Elijah had to believe for a performance, when others didn't believe or wanted to receive what he was saying about his God. One thing you can trust is that, when God's name is on the ballot, He will win every time and He's going to go over and beyond.

In life you tried your visions and ideas before, at that time it didn't work out right, but this time you won't be the one working it, but the word will work it.

Last time wasn't the time. You depended on your skills and who you knew, and how much you knew. This time it's on God and not on you or what you know.

Do not walk in fear of what happened in the past, but live in the reality that you have favor working for you now.

Receive It!
Don't overlook the blessing you already have.
The words that are in you will prosper you.
—Jekalyn Carr

Good versus Evil

I want you to understand how *good* rules in your life, but evil tries to counter act every good word that is over your life.

Bad words originated to come against the image of you being like God. Bad words were formed to make you think less of you. You must understand that you are not a cheat, liar or backbiter. You are the chosen one from the beginning. You are not your mistake. You are not your sin. You are not your errors. You are beautifully and wonderfully made by the hands of Jesus.

The good words over your life will push you to your destiny, but the evil words will rob you of your destiny. As words are being released over you and your family, you better begin to cast every evil word down and release the good word of God over your life. You must use the right words to prosper.

You have been exposed to evil. Now, God told me to tell you it's time to get you exposed to the good words that He has spoken about you, the head and not the tail, above and not beneath.

If all you ever talked about is haters, guess what? You will continue to see haters, but if you talk about the goodness that God has allowed, then you will see the good in your life manifested.

The less room you make for the negative; the positive atmosphere will take control.

It's important to stay connected to the words that God has spoken over your life and not the negative words that come to steal our joy, peace, jobs and relationships. Keep the good vibration words working for you.

PRAYER

Dear heavenly father,

Your word says, that we are more than conquerors! Your word also tells me, that you have ordained me to live the life of abundance. You created me with your word. You watch over me to perform miracles, signs and wonders! I command the healing angels, angels of victory, angels of strength, angels of motivation, empowerment, and encouragement to work around the clock! It is not your will, that we be defeated and bound by the things of this world. Provoke me to walk into a 360 breakthrough. Father, cause me to conquer every area that i've been defeated in!! Thank you, for you have lifted up a standard, so that I can have the victory!! I declare this is my winning season! When I win, everything attached to me wins!!

A Prayer for the Victorious

"Thank you, that we are no longer bound by our past and free from any curse. We are free and we can now live our lives in total victory! Thank you for giving us victory over every challenge life brings. Thank you for being with us and for giving your people great victories! Thank you for causing your people to triumph over their enemies and thank you Father, for giving us a mindset of VICTORY!

Amen."

7 Purposes of Prayer:

1. Healing
2. Release from bondage
3. Breaking generational curses
4. Worship
5. Power
6. Gratitude
7. Knowing God

Prayer Strategies

We benefit so much from prayer. As in any relationship, our connection to God, our prayer lives, must be cultivated and attended to. It should also be our goal to evolve in the prayers that we offer up. Our prayer lives should change from one year or cycle of life to the next.

To win, we must get deep into prayer We must dig deep within our souls to offer up the contents of our hearts to God during prayer.

We cannot expect results when we pray empty prayers. The monotony of life often leads us in this direction, but we must go deeper into our prayer and ask God for things that we never even imagined possible. I have witnessed in my life, the way that God blesses us when we go deeper with prayer. Just as I spoke of mediocrity in our lives, we must not allow that same spirit to creep into our prayer lives. We can never take for granted the opportunity to talk with God. Prayer changes things.

REFLECTIONS FOR VICTORY: #INTENTIONALVICTORY

Setting clear goals for what we want to achieve is a pattern for victory. Achieving our goals can be satisfying to us and pleasing to God. Use the space below to define three specific victories that you want to achieve.

Setting Goals

Victory #1

_____

_____

How will the goal be measured?

_____

_____

How will you achieve the goal?

_____

_____

How fast will you achieve the goal?

_____

_____

Victory #2

_____

_____

How will the goal be measured?

_____

_____

How will you achieve the goal?

_____

_____

How fast will you achieve the goal?

_____

_____

Victory #3

_____

_____

How will the goal be measured?

_____

_____

How will you achieve the goal?

_____

_____

How fast will you achieve the goal?

_____

_____

The Road to Winning

How do you define "win"?

_____

_____

Who can help you to be successful?

_____

_____

Why is success important to you?

_____

_____

YOU WILL WIN. YOU WILL WIN. YOU WILL WIN. YOU WILL WIN. YOU WILL WIN.

YOU WILL WIN. YOU WILL WIN. YOU WILL WIN. YOU WILL WIN. YOU WILL WIN.

YOU WILL WIN. YOU WILL WIN. YOU WILL WIN. YOU WILL WIN. YOU WILL WIN.

YOU WILL WIN. YOU WILL WIN. YOU WILL WIN. YOU WILL WIN. YOU WILL WIN. YOU WILL WIN. YOU WILL WIN. YOU WILL WIN. YOU WILL WIN. YOU WILL WIN.

YOU WILL WIN. YOU WILL WIN. YOU WILL WIN. YOU WILL WIN. YOU WILL WIN. YOU WILL WIN. YOU WILL WIN. YOU WILL WIN. YOU WILL WIN. YOU WILL WIN.

YOU WILL WIN. YOU WILL WIN. YOU WILL WIN. YOU WILL WIN. YOU WILL WIN. YOU WILL WIN. YOU WILL WIN. YOU WILL WIN. YOU WILL WIN. YOU WILL WIN.

YOU WILL WIN. YOU WILL WIN. YOU WILL WIN. YOU WILL WIN. YOU WILL WIN. YOU WILL WIN. YOU WILL WIN. YOU WILL WIN. YOU WILL WIN. YOU WILL WIN.

YOU WILL WIN. YOU WILL WIN. YOU WILL WIN. YOU WILL WIN. YOU WILL WIN. YOU WILL WIN. YOU WILL WIN. YOU WILL WIN. YOU WILL WIN. YOU WILL WIN.

YOU WILL WIN. YOU WILL WIN. YOU WILL WIN. YOU WILL WIN. YOU WILL WIN. YOU WILL WIN. YOU WILL WIN. YOU WILL WIN. YOU WILL WIN. YOU WILL WIN.

YOU WILL WIN. YOU WILL WIN. YOU WILL WIN. YOU WILL WIN. YOU WILL WIN. YOU WILL WIN. YOU WILL WIN. YOU WILL WIN. YOU WILL WIN. YOU WILL WIN.

YOU WILL WIN. YOU WILL WIN. YOU WILL WIN. YOU WILL WIN. YOU WILL WIN. YOU WILL WIN. YOU WILL WIN. YOU WILL WIN. YOU WILL WIN. YOU WILL WIN.

YOU WILL WIN. YOU WILL WIN. YOU WILL WIN. YOU WILL WIN. YOU WILL WIN. YOU WILL WIN. YOU WILL WIN. YOU WILL WIN. YOU WILL WIN. YOU WILL WIN.

You were created as a winner from birth. It is in your DNA. You were conceived in the womb as a winner. Somewhere in life, words, experiences, misunderstandings, errors, bad choices, sin, environments, emotions, feelings and unforgiveness planted all these negative ideas in you. Issues tried to mix into your blood line to alter your DNA and who you are. They tried to lock down every good thing about you. These things wanted you to be deceived so that you can live in defeat and toil. They wanted to rob you of your joy and happiness.

I wrote this book to tell you that you are not the bad thoughts and words that were trying to block your vision of who you really are. They may have tried to get in your DNA, but you were covered by the blood, and nothing can come against the blood that was shed to cover your sins so that you can WIN. Your life will change significantly for the good once you understand that it was all an illusion that was trying to discredit you. You are God's people and He loves you no matter what. Your mistake didn't define you and will not stop the blessing that is upon your life.

When you bump yourself, just say, "I am a winner!"

When you cut yourself, just say, "I am a winner!"

When you fall, get up and say, "I am a winner!"

That's who you are and nothing less.

You were born to win. You were born as a champion. You were born victorious. These are your names, live by your name and not by your experiences.

You will win!

AN OPEN LETTER

Dear Winner,

Prosperity looks good on you. I declare the abundance of love, power, grace, endurance and victory over your life as you read these words from my heart. It is my belief that we have been placed here on earth to be of service to others.

God desires for us to be prosperous in every area and phase of our life. God wants us to have Him wholeheartedly, so that we can live and flourish in prosperity. He wants us to have salvation. He wants us to have good health. He wants us to have joy, and He wants us to have peace. He took the stripes on his back that we might be healed. God took persecution so that we could live in peace. He became poor so that we might be rich. As we walk in righteousness, we are blessed. God uses the blessed to bless others. We must not question prosperity. It is a good thing, and God created it for his people. Prosperity positions us to help others.

The lifetime of joy comes from God. Things come and go. You may be happy about getting a new car today, but the joy of that new car lasts only for a short time, because months later you will be ready for a newer one. It's great to have nice things, but you must understand that *stuff* doesn't make you. As a matter of fact, you make that *stuff* look good.

You have been called to do a mighty thing in your lifetime. You are destined for abundance and greatness. Never allow anyone or anything to set limitations on what you can accomplish. You were created by a God who took the time to sculpt every detail on your body. From the hair on your head to the soles of your feet, you are wrapped in greatness. Use your mind as a tool to imagine what can be. Imagine how you can change the world. The simple fact that you woke up this morning and you are reading this letter determines that you have purpose. It is so. The question is what will you do with it? Seeds of greatness have been sown into your DNA. Keep your eyes focused on what lies ahead. Do good work in your community? Work hard to maintain an attitude of gratitude. You will be rewarded.

Know that nothing worth having comes easily, and anything that comes easily is not worth having.

What you do today determines what will manifest in your life tomorrow. Sow seeds of greatness.

Never forget to listen to wise council. Those who have won before you and lived life longer, know what it takes to win. Seek them out and listen to them. Learn from those who have already gone where you desire to go.

When you feel joy in your heart, know that it is God and go closer to it. You will find your purpose rooted there. Take time to let your face feel the warmth of the sunlight and watch the wind blow the leaves of the trees. The simple things in life are the ones that we so often take for granted, but you will find abounding peace there.

Pay close attention to your spirit of discernment. It is your GPS that helps to determine what is wrong and what is right. It is your internal guide. Use it. Never forget that your words have power to create whatever you want to happen in your life.

Heed the voice of God; it is real and all knowing.

Commit to excellence.

Do everything well and with good intentions and remember that God loves you and so do I.

Written with Love,
Jekalyn Carr

ABOUT THE AUTHOR

I grew up in a Christian home in West Memphis, Arkansas, with my parents, brother, Allen Carr Jr., my sister Allundria Carr, and my god-sister, Nariah Smith. We attended church where one of my uncle's pastored. Later, when my father received the calling to ministry, we attended the ministry under my father.

Before I started singing professionally, I was doing a lot of singing locally and this was part of my preparation. God was getting me ready — giving me a glimpse of where He was leading me.

I loved hymns and my favorite song to sing back then was "Amazing Grace".

God can use you no matter what age you are. Even at a young age, I loved singing to crowds. It always brought me joy, because singing is a part of me, being able to share with people and inspire people though my music, made me smile. At that age, I told God all I wanted was to give people hope and to inspire them through my gift.

As a little girl, I knew that one day I would be great. My messages have always been inspirational. In my music, speaking, and now my writing. I want to uplift people, inspire people, and push people to that place where God intends for them to be.

I thought that singing was my only calling, but when I was about 13, God started to speak to me and say, "There is more that I require of you." I really didn't understand what God was saying, but He spoke again, saying, "There is more that I require of you. You are to teach." So, he ushered me into my calling of preaching.

BIOGRAPHY OF JEKALYN CARR

Jekalyn Carr is a dynamic singer, preacher, and speaker. Carr was busy spending her teen years traveling the globe and building a multi-media motivational empire. Singing professionally since the age of 15, and public-speaking before that, Carr, now 20 years old - a Grammy and Billboard Music Award nominee and Stellar Award winner - has recently expanded her reach by filming her debut television and film roles, authoring her first book, and spending a half-decade at the top of the music charts.

Carr burst onto the Gospel music scene in 2013 with the poignant and powerful single, "Greater Is Coming." The single was released independently on her family owned label, Lunjeal Music Group, and immediately showcased a vocal ability and intensity far beyond her 15 years. "Greater Is Coming" ultimately reached Top 5 on the Billboard charts, and established Carr as one to watch. Carr's first Billboard #1 album "The Life Project" and #1 single "You're Bigger" came at the age of 19, respectively, and yielded other monumental firsts for Carr, as an independent artist. The single, which was named the #2 most played Gospel song in 2016 by Billboard Magazine.

2017 has found Carr in front of the camera, as well as behind the microphone, in a critically lauded cameo appearance during Season 2 of OWN Network's hit original series, *Greenleaf*, as well as in her debut film role, in which she shares the screen with such dramatic and pop culture icons as Robin Givens, Brian White, David Banner, Kandi Burruss, and many more, in the forthcoming 2018 release, *I Never Heard My Father Speak*. In both roles, Carr has delivered captivating and engaging performances while standing alongside legends in the fields of television and film, respectively.

This past year has also added another hyphen to her already impressive list of titles and accomplishments, as she became an "author" for the first time with the announcement of her first book, You Will Win: Inspirational Strategies to Help You Overcome. In the book, published in association with Trinity Broadcasting Network's international publishing arm, and scheduled for wide release in early 2018, Carr offer motivational and inspirational tips and tactics to empower readers to overcome the obstacles of life and to live victoriously.

Included in the book are snippets of her motivational talks that she has delivered over the years as well as fresh, new approaches to successful living.

The book will coincide with the release of Carr's fourth album, One Nation Under God.

The new album features a lead single that shares its name with that of her book, "You Will Win," and that has already ascended to the coveted Top 10 on the elusive and fiercely competitive radio charts. "You Will Win" is a powerful message, encouraging listeners that they have all the tools needed for victory, already inside of them. One Nation Under God is the highly anticipated follow-up to Carr's Number 1 album, The Life Project, which features the Number 1 single, "You Are Bigger," and which garnered her aforementioned Grammy and Billboard Music Award nominations.

2018 is shaping up to be a dynamic year for Carr, as she continued to make her mark, across many mediums and platforms.

Remember this is "YOUR WINNING SEASON"

I WANT TO REITERATE THIS TO YOU

You were "CREATED TO WIN"
Your "WINNING SEASON" is not compared to the four seasons of the earth; summer, fall, winter or spring, but it is a set time of being victorious.

"IT'S A SEASON THAT'S LASTS A LIFETIME".
"ENJOY YOUR LIFETIME OF WINNING"
"FAILURE IS NOT IN YOUR DNA"
"YOU HAVE WINNING WORDS OVER LIFE"
"YOU ARE A CHAMPION"
"GOD DON'T BIRTH NO FAILURES"
"SPEAK SUCCESS"
"GREATER IS COMING"

"SOMETHING BIG IS HAPPENING"
"LIVE BEYOND YOUR PAST"
"YOUR FUTURE IS A WINNING FUTURE"

I leave you with this..............

YOU WILL WIN. YOU WILL WIN. YOU WILL WIN. YOU WILL WIN. YOU WILL WIN. YOU WILL WIN. YOU WILL WIN. YOU WILL WIN. YOU WILL WIN. YOU WILL WIN.

YOU WILL WIN. YOU WILL WIN. YOU WILL WIN. YOU WILL WIN. YOU WILL WIN.

YOU WILL WIN. YOU WILL WIN. YOU WILL WIN. YOU WILL WIN. YOU WILL WIN. YOU WILL WIN. YOU WILL WIN. YOU WILL WIN. YOU WILL WIN. YOU WILL WIN.

YOU WILL WIN. YOU WILL WIN. YOU WILL WIN. YOU WILL WIN. YOU WILL WIN. YOU WILL WIN. YOU WILL WIN. YOU WILL WIN. YOU WILL WIN. YOU WILL WIN.

YOU WILL WIN. YOU WILL WIN. YOU WILL WIN. YOU WILL WIN. YOU WILL WIN. YOU WILL WIN. YOU WILL WIN. YOU WILL WIN. YOU WILL WIN. YOU WILL WIN.

YOU WILL WIN. YOU WILL WIN. YOU WILL WIN. YOU WILL WIN. YOU WILL WIN. YOU WILL WIN. YOU WILL WIN. YOU WILL WIN. YOU WILL WIN. YOU WILL WIN.

YOU WILL WIN. YOU WILL WIN. YOU WILL WIN. YOU WILL WIN. YOU WILL WIN. YOU WILL WIN. YOU WILL WIN. YOU WILL WIN. YOU WILL WIN. YOU WILL WIN.

YOU WILL WIN. YOU WILL WIN. YOU WILL WIN. YOU WILL WIN. YOU WILL WIN. YOU WILL WIN. YOU WILL WIN. YOU WILL WIN. YOU WILL WIN. YOU WILL WIN.

YOU WILL WIN. YOU WILL WIN. YOU WILL WIN. YOU WILL WIN. YOU WILL WIN. YOU WILL WIN. YOU WILL WIN. YOU WILL WIN. YOU WILL WIN. YOU WILL WIN.

YOU WILL WIN. YOU WILL WIN. YOU WILL WIN. YOU WILL WIN. YOU WILL WIN. YOU WILL WIN. YOU WILL WIN. YOU WILL WIN. YOU WILL WIN. YOU WILL WIN.

A few years ago, my family and I had an amazing vacation to Washington, D.C., the District of Columbia. While there, we had the most excellent opportunity to visit the National Air and Space Museum. With bewilderment, we were educated about our awe-inspiring and miraculous Universe (the planets, outer space, the sun and the galaxies.) As we walked around viewing the exhibits and presentations, there was one remarkable display that had me at a pause, which was a planetarium. There, we had the joy of leaning far back in the reclining chairs enjoying such an astounding view. We were able to see the true vastness of our Universe as though it was within hands reach.

In this, I learned how immense the Universe is. No matter where you are, from any point of the world, you can only see a narrow part of the universe. The Universe is so vast that you can't see it all from one place, even with all the sophisticated and highly advanced equipment we have in this world. I realized the only one eye could see all the planets, galaxies, and constellations, and that is the eye of God.

The observation remained with me for days and even weeks after. I continued to conversate how vast the Universe is. Our God is more prominent, and He will forever be. Months later, my dad, Allen Carr Sr, had conferences to attend. When he returned, he explained how something regarding the discussion was vexing his spirit, because how the people were having hard times. He then stated, "God has given me this song because He has heard the cries of the people. God wants His people to know how big He is."

My dad began to sing:
You're bigger than the universe
You're bigger than the Sun and the stars
You're bigger than the things
That can tear me apart....
For I know, You're great in all the earth
For I know, You're great in all the earth
You're bigger...."

May 2016, God gave my father this song, but it wasn't until September 2016 when God directed us to record, You're Bigger." On October 22, 2016, we had a live recording, entitled "The Life Project," which featured the song, "You're Bigger."

Little did we know this song would touch the world and have such a significant impact on everyone. "You're Bigger" addresses the issues people of this world are troubled with daily, such as financial needs, sickness, marital breakdowns, etc. The goal of this song is to turn the people's minds from their issues and back to our God who created all things and who is bigger than anything you can imagine. He's bigger than cancer. He's bigger than diabetes. He's bigger than HIV.; He's bigger than depression. He's bigger than negativity. He's bigger He's *bigger, bigger, bigger, bigger, bigger.*

The message I want to convey to His people is when you have God's people in your heart; He will give you words whether in sermons, songs, written, or any other way to reach and build His people.

MY GREATEST INSPIRATION IS WATCHING PEOPLE SUCCEED AND FLOURISH TO THEIR GREATEST POTENTIALS IN LIFE.

YOU WILL WIN!

JEKALYN CARR

At Some Point Every Champion Takes A Blow
But What Matters The Most
Is When You Get Back Up And Fight
And Not Only Fight,
But Win Your Fight!!!
—Jekalyn Carr

Follow me on all social media outlets:

Twitter	Instagram	Facebook
@jekalyncarr	@jekalyncarr	@jekalyncarr

CPSIA information can be obtained
at www.ICGtesting.com
Printed in the USA
LVOW13s0622070318
568967LV00028B/416/P